Just Go And Do It.

By Michael Lennon

copyright © 2004 Michael Lennon

Cover – The Sam Maguire Cup on display when the 2003 All-Ireland Champions Tyrone visited Boston. In March 2004, Boston was one of the cities to be visited by the team, lead by Tyrone Captain, Peter Canavan, County Board Officials Frank Campbell and Culbert Donnelly.

Stories Adapted To Book Form By.. Dan Hallissey

© Copyright 2004 Michael Lennon.
All rights reserved. No part of this publication may be reproduced, stored in a retrieval system, or transmitted, in any form or by any means, electronic, mechanical, photocopying, recording, or otherwise, without the written prior permission of the author.

Note for Librarians: a cataloguing record for this book that includes Dewey Decimal Classification and US Library of Congress numbers is available from the Library and Archives of Canada. The complete cataloguing record can be obtained from their online database at:
www.collectionscanada.ca/amicus/index-e.html
ISBN 1-4120-4368-9
Printed in Victoria, BC, Canada

TRAFFORD

Offices in Canada, USA, Ireland, UK and Spain
This book was published *on-demand* in cooperation with Trafford Publishing. On-demand publishing is a unique process and service of making a book available for retail sale to the public taking advantage of on-demand manufacturing and Internet marketing. On-demand publishing includes promotions, retail sales, manufacturing, order fulfilment, accounting and collecting royalties on behalf of the author.

Book sales for North America and international:
Trafford Publishing, 6E–2333 Government St.,
Victoria, BC V8T 4P4 CANADA
phone 250 383 6864 (toll-free 1 888 232 4444)
fax 250 383 6804; email to orders@trafford.com

Book sales in Europe:
Trafford Publishing (UK) Ltd., Enterprise House, Wistaston Road Business Centre, Wistaston Road, Crewe, Cheshire CW2 7RP UNITED KINGDOM
phone 01270 251 396 (local rate 0845 230 9601)
facsimile 01270 254 983; orders.uk@trafford.com

Order online at:
www.trafford.com/robots/04-2176.html

10 9 8 7 6 5 4

A Smile.

A smile costs nothing, but gives much. It enriches them who receive, without making poorer those who give.

It takes but a moment, yet the memory of it may last forever

A smile creates happiness in the home, fosters goodwill in business and is the sign of friendship.

It brings rest to the weary, cheer to the discouraged, sunshine to the sad and is nature's best antidote to trouble.

Yet a smile cannot be bought, begged, borrowed or stolen, for it is something of no value to anyone, unless it is given away.

Some people are too tired to give you a smile. Give them one of yours. No one needs a smile so much as them who have none to give.

Introduction.

I have written this book in two distinct parts, the Irish section followed by the USA section and when you read it, I hope that there are some parts of it that you'll enjoy and maybe even have a laugh.

The book is about parts of my life and goes over some of the things I have done, or in some cases, tried to do. To some people, it seems I never worked a day in my life and to others, they think I've never stopped working.

Without the help of many people, I certainly would not have got as much done. If ever there was a time that I needed assistance in any way, there were a few good men that would always go out of their way to help me and they were Patsy O' Connor, from Kilmaine, Co. Mayo, George Ingram, who hails from Salt Lake City, Utah and Dan Hallissey, from Cork.

With Patsy O Connor, no matter what one was trying to do, his answer was always the same 'I cannot see why it would not work'. Likewise with George Ingram, there was never anything he did not know how to do.

Dan Hallissey also was always there to help out with web design, printing and without his help, this book would never have been created. All of these men have been the source of the greatest help to me, down through the years.

A special mention of some long time friends Francie Donoghue R.I.P., Sean Regan and Michael Flynn, all from Roscommon.

Another character worthy of mention would be, Vinny Mawn who helped out countless Irish lads in the Seventies and Eighties. Fair play to you, Vinny.

I would like to give a special thanks to Frank Flannery of the Eglington Hotel and to Mr. & Mrs. Dan Ryan, who gave me my first place to operate and work out of so many years ago. Also thanks goes to Mary Flannery and Pat McGovern for their help at all times. Also Eilish and Kevin at Lonegan's, Tom and Jimmie Kiloran, Tommie & Linda Keyes, Seamus Nestor, Joe Quinn, Mrs. Donohue, Theresa Burke, Jimmy Logue, Maura Griffin, Frank Hoye, Pat Bratten and Supt. Michael Curley and his Men for their help and curiosity down through the years

Finally, this book would not have been possible without the help and guidance from Ann Phelan and Francis Lennon over the many years.

Thank you very much.
Michael

Quotes Of Interest.

Down through the years, there have been a few quotes that I've heard and remembered and there's a story behind each one. I've included some of them here in this book. For example, did you know, it takes a smart man to tell a lie, a fool better tell the truth. The cruelest thing that a man can do to another man who takes his wife, is to leave her to him. When you're self employed, you work twenty four hours a day but you get to pick your time off.

A good settlement is when nobody is happy leaving the table. Everything that can be said has already been said but since everyone has not been listening, you can say it again. If I had known I was going to live this long, I would have taken better care of myself when I was young. A woman needs a man only when the car wouldn't start and there's a mouse about the house. Behind every good man there's a woman but behind every good woman there's no man.

John has borrowed a million, say a prayer for him - I would say a prayer for the person that gave it to him. I can give you everything you ever wanted except waste your time. A small leak can sink a large ship. Hey you, white man, you are the devil. When Clinton lied, nobody died. A confession for everyone when they reach thirty, everything to be forgotten, a clean start for everyone. We only remember what we want to remember.

When you reach fifty be prepared to pay for everything. Eating is just a mean old habit, how could you be hungry Saturday after eating all week? What does it tell you about a man that opens the door of a car for a lady, it's either a new car or a new woman. Every young man is the best driver and the best lover in the world, in his own mind. The more you think of something, the less likely it's going to be right.

We were told that when we were young that hard work had never killed anyone, that was a lie. If I had known that things would have worked out this way, I'd have picked the cotton myself. A pedestrian may be a man paying for two cars, one for his wife and one for his son or daughter. Inside every fat person, there's a thin person waiting to get out.

When you point your finger at someone, just remember, there's three more pointing back at you. You can be dead right and still be dead. What's courage?, courage to admit that you are wrong. Political talk is shooting from the lip. You get out of life what you put into it.

Did the wealthy man leave much money and property, when he died? He left everything, he took nothing with him.

I can't do that – probably means that I don't want to do it and lastly, don't every refuse money, you'll never know when you might need it.

Ireland Of Today.

The old country is no longer the old country. You could spend a long time looking for the old ways, however, the first problem would be to find anyone that knew what you were talking about. The Celtic Tiger that started about 10 years ago attracted many new people to the country, some came here to work, while others came for a long term holiday. In most shops, bars and restaurants, you are most likely going to be served by someone with little or no English. As a result, now-a-days, you should always try to go somewhere that has self-service. I was recently looking for a weekly paper called 'Buy & Sell' and since I could not find it myself, I asked the shop assistant if she had that particular magazine. 'Yes', was her answer, 'how many do you want?', 'One, says I' and she went away and brought me back a Bottle of Bulmers cider!.

The New Ireland we have now is hard to understand for anyone that tried to make a living here in the 70's or 80's and then decided that they had to leave in order to make a living somewhere else. In particular, I remember a man that was working hard doing a bit of building. He worked from early morning until late at night everyday but unfortunately, he not able to survive since people were not paying him for the work he had completed. It eventually came to a stage where he had enough and decided to go where thousands had gone before him. He was heading off for John Bull's Land, as it was known and as he was about to leave, a man arrived and presented him with plans and drawings for a new house to be built. The man asked him to stay, saying that there'd be work there for him for six months. He replied, and many thousands of others can relate to this also, "I was never short of work, it's the money, I was short of." He went to London and stayed there for the best part of twenty years and he did very well for himself.

With the Celtic Tiger calling, he has now returned to Ireland. The changing times has seen a return of many people from England and America. New Towns are now being built where once stood small villages that only had a few houses, a shop, a church and maybe a school. Now with all the building, it's a few hundred houses, a hotel and maybe a by-pass road. This has not happened in one place but it's going on all over the country. You'll find prosperity now everywhere, you'll see young and old driving new cars, young people in there 20's, men and women owning their own house or apartment. The new trend now also seems to be, not just to own one house but two or three. This is the progress today in the old country and long may it continue. One can only be proud of the young people of Ireland now.

The way of life has changed in Ireland. It's now faster and the 'things need to be done yesterday' attitude is found everywhere. The days of 'I have such a thing to do today but sure as there's none of tomorrow gone yet, it can wait' is long gone.

School Days.

School days in the 60's and 70's were not happy ones. At that time, the word 'understanding' was not in the English Language. You would be verbally and or physically abused regularly for the most minor of offences such as forgetting homework or indeed anything at all.

You started out for school walking and carrying a sod or two of turf for the fire. This was to keep the Teacher warm and you'd better have a good nose to smell the heat, because you were not going to get near that fire. The Teacher sat with their back to the fire all day long and the only heat you got was from Teacher's Mouth. If you were caught talking in class you would be beaten and verbally abused and you would be told something like 'Empty vessels made the most noise'.

If asked something that you did not know, you dared not say 'I don't know', it would be better just say nothing at all and wait. The classroom would be brought to attention by the Teacher roaring something like 'look at the dummy, look, two eyes that look like burned holes in a blanket' and that then could be followed by slaps or punches. On top of that, if you cried, the Teacher might say something comforting like 'look at that face, it's like a full moon in the fog'.

Whenever you cried, you would be reminded that if you did not learn, you would not be able to read or write. You then would have to rely on the good pupils at home to read you your letters. You would also be reminded that the good students were going to be in the 'Civil Service' where they'd have good jobs working forty eight hours a week, forty eight weeks a year and after forty eight years, you'd then have the pension and could retire.

Many thousands could not stay at home and remember, immigration in those days was the only way to survive. One of the main places to go would have been England or as our Teacher used to say 'you will all be going to John Bulls Land'. Unfortunately, that Teacher was right. Some did well there and since you did not need a degree to dig or build, it was through hard work that you got your money and then that translated into you making a decent living for yourself. Unfortunately, most of those people did not get the credit they deserved. Leaving home at the age of sixteen or seventeen and going to a large city put huge burden and pressure on a person of such a young age.

Now that the wheel has come full circle, people are coming back to work in Ireland. It's not unusual to be served at the shop counter by someone with an English or Foreign accent. It is good that Ireland is now in a position to provide work to foreigners and especially to the English. The tide has turned since that was, for so long our only place of employment.

The final words from our Teacher everyday, when you were going home was 'Let nobody come to school tomorrow without there homework completed, because if they do, skin and hair will be flying'. That unfortunately was something we had to look forward to.

Serving Mass.

One way to avoid time from attending School was to help out in the serving of Mass. In those days, it was not that easy as the Mass was conducted in Latin and that took some time to learn. Unfortunately, a lot of the Priests were from the same school as the Teachers and they had very little patience for anyone.

After weeks and sometimes months of been trained, which usually would include been yelled at and sometimes even punched, you might finally make it to serving Mass on a Sunday. To some of us, that was like playing in an All-Ireland Final. I will always remember long ago, a visiting Priest who was back on holidays from the USA. After serving the Mass for him, he turns around and said 'Thank You'. To this day, I am still in shock from those kind words from that Priest.

Once you had made it to serving Mass on a Sunday you might graduate and be promoted to serving at the Stations. This was a Mass that would have been held every so often in a different house in each locality. Mass was said and then breakfast was provided for the priest and the neighbors. You being the Mass Server got yourself a fine breakfast and sometimes even an apple but the best part of it all was, and everything perfectly legal too, that you missed out on school for a couple of hours. Eventually however, you had to return to that domain of horror.

Some of the pupils going to school came up with the idea of not talking at all at school. They went silent from once they left their house in the morning and remained that way throughout the day at school. The Teachers tried to make them talk but for the most part those students ended up in tears especially when they were threatened to be tied up and thrown into the lake and drowned.

Jobs During School.

Any jobs available during our school years were usually via a local Farmer. The job could be anything from sowing potatoes, picking stones, picking the potatoes again to making hay. The fun attached to the picking of potatoes was to see, who was the fastest picking them. At the time it seemed to be great fun.

Payment was usually in the form of an evening meal but in some rare cases the Farmer would say something like 'I will see you after 2nd. Mass on Sunday and I'll give you some money or I'll see your mother. However, often a problem might arise and the Farmer would finish up going to the first Mass, which meant that you missed out on getting paid. But luckily, there was always another Sunday and perhaps there would have been another chance at getting a few shillings.

I remember once been told by a farmer that he was thinking of giving me £5.00. Now at that time, that was a lot of money, enough to buy a couple of sheep so I asked him, why are you giving me the £5.00, that's a lot of money. He replied 'you were not listening to me, I said, "I was thinking of giving you £5" Needless to say, to this day, he is still thinking of it.

Picking stones was another exciting job. Usually this would come about when new ground was being prepared for a meadow, what you did or did not pick up, would not show for a few months. When the meadow was then cut, it is only then that you'd see what stones were picked and what was not. The man cutting the meadow would be complaining about blades that he broke. 'The two young lads picked every stone except one or two'. 'I think it was one or two that they picked' would have been the reply.

Then there were jobs that you might be encouraged to do but might not always pay as well as you expected. What you expected to be paid and what you got were often totally different. One such job was cutting scallops for thatching. It was easy to get started, basically get a knife and start cutting. Now the equipment supplied would not exactly be of a surgical sharpness quality so the first things to appear would have been blisters on the hands. You'd be told that they'd soon be gone and you'd be fine. What you were not told is that you'd be dead a while before they would go.

Now, I remember cutting over one thousand scallops, that would be ten bundles with one hundred in each bundle. The price that I understood was going to be five shillings a bundle, and that would make a total of £2-10-0 (two pounds, ten shillings). Now my thinking was that that would have been enough money to get started in some other venture. I soon learned that there was a mistake in the pricing, it turned out to be one shilling a bundle. Therefore, I was to get a total of 10 shillings. The £2 part was a clerical error and as the agreement was not written down, I just had to take what I got. An early lesson that was well learnt.

So with my ten shillings, what would my next business venture be ? Well, after some senior advise, it was recommended to me that I should grow some cabbage. So accordingly, cabbage seed was purchased and sewn. The cabbage plants were soon growing and things were looking good. Since there was a man near us doing very well in the same business and was getting rich fast selling cabbage and carrots, I thought that I was looking at a dead cert. The cabbage was growing well and it looked mighty until one morning, some cattle broke in and had a party. That incident resulted in a severe set back on the profits from that enterprise. From there on in, the cabbage business did not appeal to me and the other man continued to prosper and good luck to him.

The Bog.

This was another job that went on for a few months every year. It was hard work no doubt and not alone had you a job at cutting your own turf but you would also be in the firing line of the neighbors when they called for your help. The work started with the cleaning the turf bank and that entailed removing the top, the heather and whatever else needed to be removed to get at the turf below. It was then ready for cutting. One man would cut out the turf while you would catch it as he cut it out. You then had to put it on a wheel barrow and wheeled it over to some dry ground. You then went back for some more and that job usually went on for days. Once that was done, then you spread it out for drying.

After a week or more, you turned it again for the weather to dry it. When the turf was about half dry, you would then put it into small heaps and these would be later be removed to the road beside the bog where it would remain for a few more weeks to be completely dried out. The next move then would be to take the turf home on a horse and cart or in later years, by tractor and trailer. This was labor intensive work since every sod of turf had to be put onto the cart, brought home, dropped off on the ground and then put inside the shed. With Winter setting in and the turf piled up in the shed, all that was left to do was to burn it.

You were not finished yet, as a final act to this saga, you needed to put it into a bag and then take that into the house. With the turf burning, it was then time to sit back and relax and enjoy the fruits of your hard work. You would feel the heat and watch it burn and when the lovely sods of turf, that you had handled at least ten times, was extinguished, the fire was now in ashes so you had one last final act to do. That was to remove the ashes from the fireplace and that then would finally be the end of the turf job. What a world of work for such little return.

You would be expected to do that work for your neighbors too and for not much more payment than food, maybe a fry of bacon and eggs with fried bread with tea gravy. For those of you watching your cholesterol, I'd advise avoiding the tea gravy.

This was made by pouring tea into the pan after the bacon was fried in it, this now was at a time before Bisto became popular and I'm sure that whatever cholesterol was in that brew, was of the bad variety.

Today, the turf cutting process is much less labor intensive as machines have replaced the cutting. However, it's still a lot of work for very little of return in the form of some heat and lots of ashes.

Bringing Home The Animals.

Working with different farmers brought on different jobs, some would entail picking potatoes, celery or beet but one of the easier jobs would be the bringing the cattle or sheep from one farm to another. One such Farmer that I used to work for had some livestock on another farm that was many miles on the other side of the Town from the farm that he had lived all his life.

Now he had the cattle there grazing for some time and when they were due to be returned back to the farmer's home place, getting them home proved to be a much more of a difficult task than taking them there. The trouble was getting through the local town, traffic was not a factor since there were few cars around at that time and road works were few and far between. However, something that was not few or far between was the Pubs.

Every day for about two weeks, we could not pass through the town without saying hello to his friends. That hello would then develop into a long conversation and it would be evening and many pints before goodbyes would be said and it being time to go home.

The greeting from his Wife would be the same every evening. She'd ask 'How did you get on with the cattle? Did you get them home all right,?' 'No' says the Farmer, 'one of them was sick but sure I'm sure it will be better tomorrow. We'll go again then'. The following day, the same story. After going through many different excuses, sick cow, slippery road and the like, the cattle made it home eventually.

It nearly came to the stage where the Wife had to wait for the cattle and cows to come home on their own accord.

Cattle & Sheep Fairs.

If you were lucky enough to be asked by a neighbor to take his cattle or sheep to a local Fair, you were fast becoming a man. You'd have to get up out of bed around three in the morning. That was followed then by a three or four hours walk with the animals to the Fair. The idea was to have the animals pinned in and ready by six or seven in the morning in order to get the best price when the Buyers had money to spend.

The Buyers would come and have a look and eventually the animals would be sold. Then it's off to the pub with the Buyer and Seller where many hours would be spent in the company of Arthur Guinness while junior would be left minding the flock. By four or five o'clock in the evening the exchange of monies would have taken place. Once the handover was complete, you'd be finally done with the fair. You usually got paid well for the long day. There'd be none of the 'I'll see you Sunday after second Mass' since the Farmer had the cash in hand and the Guinness had made his grip on it less severe. In comparison to the cabbage or turf, Fair days were good.

Extermination Of Vermin.

There was a very good way for school children to make money if you were not a great animal lover and this job included killing foxes, badgers, grey crows and magpies. You would have gotten a reward for each one you killed. I don't know who came up with this, but it was certainly going to keep you busy following grey crows and magpies around the place. However, trying to kill them by throwing stones at them was not a very lucrative method of making money.

With little or no success for these young bounty hunters, it was decided to change the rules a little to make it a bit easier to build up a catch of vermin. It was allowed to let them catch the birds in the nests. As soon as there were feathers growing, you could move in for the kill. This cruel practice operated for a while, upon successful kills, you took your catch to the Garda Station, then filled out a form and sent it away. You then waited for the check to come. However, I don't think anyone ever got paid which, in my mind was the right thing to happen.

Foxes and badgers was a much better paying job, much harder to catch but the rewards were greater. There was a bounty of five shillings for each animal killed and that was a lot of money at the time. I remember after two days of hunting with nothing to show a well meaning older hunter was feeling sorry for me, he told me that there was a fox dead in an outhouse and suggested that I take it to the barracks to get the five shillings for it. Delighted with that act of kindness, I put the fox in a sack bag and off I went to the Garda Barracks. When I arrived there, the Sergeant asked what did I have and where did I get it. 'A Fox', says I, 'and I got him in the bog'.

Now unknown to me at the time, the only proof you needed to get your money was that the tongue or tale was cut off and the rest of the animal be dumped. Now this fox was a big fellow, it had an extra long tail. In fact, I was thinking this one might even be worth more than the usual five shillings.
The sergeant commented that 'this was a fine fox' and that he may have seen him before. 'Open his mouth there', says the Sergeant. I open his mouth, no tongue. The Sergeant said that he didn't think I should have killed him because with no tongue, he was harmless and could eat nothing.

As things turned out, the Good Samaritan that gave me the fox had already taken him to the barracks and got paid for him. The Sergeant, knowing that I was set up, told me to wait a minute. He gave me a form to fill out and to make a claim, which was nice of him to do. I hope that whatever Government

Department that was paying me has recovered from that loss by now.

The Rosary.

There would be an attempt made every evening to say the Rosary at home. Sometimes, it would be dedicated to the speedy recovery of a sick cow or calf and on those evenings, successful completion of the prayers would be assured. I remember one time, it was once offered for the safe return of the neighbor's ducks. Unfortunately our prayer were not answered since the ducks were found dead about two days later.

In around that same time, there were men that used to call themselves fowlers. They would be men with guns and they'd be out hunting but after a long day out shooting and nothing to show for it, they turned their anger and frustration on the local pond. Anything that moved on the water was a target.

All the Rosaries in the World could not bring the ducks back to life and it's possible that the phrase 'Sitting Dick' came forth from that episode.

When the rosary did start, it would be said with the full unedited version of the 'Hail Mary' but after four or five repetitions, it would begin to be cut shorter and eventually it would be abbreviated to just only 'Hail Mary, Holy Mary, Mother of God'. Now and again, the concentration would be broken with a 'did you close the hen house door? That bloody fox will eat the chickens, say a prayer for their safety also'.

The next question to be asked would be something like, 'was that the third or fourth mystery?' someone would answer 'the fifth' and immediately tear into 'Hail Holy Queen, Mother of Mercy, check the chickens and see that the fox didn't get any of them.'

During the Week, many Chickens were saved by reciting the Rosary but on the Weekends, it was not unusual for one of them to appear on the table for Sunday Dinner. The fox being cleared of all charges.

There ends the Rosary, Amen.

The Missions.

This was a special treat when the Mission Priests would come to the local Church for a week. They would say Mass each and every evening followed by a long Sermon. Now this was intended to bring you back in line with the faith and keep you straightened on the road to Heaven.

The Mission Priests worked as a pair. One would be quite and very reverend while the other did all the roaring, threatening you with hell and all the consequences that went along with it. Each night there would be a different sermon, one night it would be on the importance of Confession and Holy Communion, the next would be on what was called 'company keeping' and a stern warning about looking at other men's wives. It was stressed that the Commandment clearly said 'Though shall not covet thy neighbor's Wife'. Oddly enough, we took great relief when we realized that it said nothing about his daughters.

On other nights, the Sermon would be focused upon the evils of alcohol. Now the week's sermons would be announced on the previous Sunday and the subject of these Sermons would be told in advance. In our Parish, as in many others, there was a certain amount of men who liked more than their fair share of the drink and they usually planned on not being there for the sermon. They considered those Sermons to be boring. On an totally unrelated matter, the craic in the pubs on those nights was mighty.

The local parishioners had their schedule already made out between alcohol devilment and company keeping, now called living together. However, throughout the years, the Mission Priests had noticed a major drop off in attendance on the nights that the sermon about alcohol was due for airing. On this particular occasion, Wednesday was scheduled in for the sermon on company keeping. On that night, all the seats near the front of the alter were full with all the experienced drinkers from the Community. With their ears perked up, waiting to be enlightened on the joys of company keeping and all that goes with it, a spanner was thrown in the works when there was a last minute change in the Sermon schedule.

The Mission Priests knew right well that they had trawled in a prime catch of well established drinkers on that night and they laced into the evils of alcohol. With the priest roaring out on the top of his voice what drink has done to Families and how drink paves the road to Hell and anybody who drinks will never see the face of God. He pointed to the front row and told then that they were all going to Hell.

Now this unexpected sermon was taking its toll. They had heard enough but there was no let up, the missioner knew that he had put the fear of God into them and after much preaching and scorning he then offered them a chance at salvation. Confessions were to be heard and anyone who repented and paid penance would, upon death be greeted by Angels at the Gates of Heaven and taken directly to the Man above.

The Priest roared 'Will the first man that wants to start out on the road to heaven, stand up and be counted'. Moments, which seemed like an eternity passed, no one stood up. Then the Priest then started all over again on the evils of drink telling them that how 'he knew first hand about the evils and how his own brother was an alcoholic and where is he now? - He is in hell. He is burning in hell. He'll be there forever, eternity and there's no way out. He is going to be there forever and all because of alcohol'.

At this stage the poor drinkers at the front of the alter had enough and could not listen to him anymore. They stood up and started to walk out. The Missioner roared at them 'You are going to go to hell, the place where my brother is'. With that, one of men who was walking out turns around and shouts back, 'have you got any message for him'.

That was the end of Wednesday's Sermon.

Petrol Pump Money.

Once I found out about money and learned how to count it, it was time for me to go out and get some. I remembered that it seemed unlikely that cutting scallops or market gardening was going to be the way to make my fortune. Also, the 'I'll see you after 2nd. Mass' line wasn't working out too well either. It was time to look for some work in the nearest town which meant leaving school early. The only qualifications that I had was that I knew I had to go to 'John Bulls Land' to start work but even to do that, I needed some money.

At the petrol station, the pay was £1-10-0 a week. During the twelve months that I was there, I never was able to get that full amount. I was always a few pence short, which would be taken out of the £1-10-0. At that time, the hours were from nine to six and I worked six days a week. The hourly rate was fairly low and therefore saving any amount of money for any new project that one might be planning would have been very difficult.

To make an extra few shilling, I sometimes drained almost half empty oil cans into other oil cans when you sold a half pint or so, selling them on then turned out to be a nice little earner. The usual order was five shillings of petrol and sometimes a half pint or a pint of Castrol GTX 20-30. Now and again, you might have the rich people getting ten shillings worth for Angela. The old lads used to name the Anglia car 'Angela'. That was the name the old Anglia was called and ten shillings I am sure, nearly filled her. I saw a car recently that took over €100 of petrol to fill her.

You know, oil is valuable and the World keeps going on using oil. When oil was first pumped out of the ground in Texas, some smart people were asking 'what are they going to do with it? Feed it to the horses!'

The Television.

The introduction of the television into our lives was something always to be remembered. The first TV's to appear would have been in the late fifties and the BBC programs were all that were available. RTE came on the air in early sixties. The picture was black and white and the programs only ran for a few hours every night.

The main event for most of the Country was the Angelus and the News. Such programs like 'The Virginian', 'Voyage To The Bottom Of The Sea', 'Maxwell Smart' and '99' were a big hit. The most watched show every week with everyone at the edge of their seats was 'The Fugitive'. Would he be caught this week? if he was, that would have been the end of it. There was no program reviews available at that time. But with everyone praying for his escape (some Rosaries were offered up, I'm sure) that meant that he could continue and he always got away.

Somehow, I don't think that the detective following him, Lieutenant Gerard, would have ever got a warm 'Cead Mile Failte' in Ireland. The fugitive was hunted for the murder of his wife, he had been tried by the TV audience and was acquitted. So there was no need to keep following him.

After many years of escaping his popularity was eventually overtaken by Benjy, Maggie and Tom of the Riordians. Then you had Bunny Carr and Quicksilver and so on. Today we have the likes of 'Fair City' and 'Who Wants to be A Millionaire'.

Moving To Dublin.

Moving to Dublin City in the Sixties was a major event for me. Being from the Country, there were a lot of things there that I was not familiar with, even the Double Decker buses looked strange to me. I remember been told to watch out for the toilets when you go there. I was told, you 'pull a string and in a jiffy, it goes sailing down the Liffey'.

When you get there you probably stayed with someone you knew for a week or more and then found what was called a flat or bed-sit. The cost then was £3 or £4 per week. There, you slept, ate, watched TV and all in the one room. The toilet and bathroom would be shared by the other tenants in the bed-sitters on that floor. This was a new life and a new found freedom.

If you liked Dublin, then there were so many places to go. If you did not care too much for it, there were always the weekend trips to the Country Estate. Dublin in the Sixties and Seventies were full of nightclubs and dance halls, there were more than fifty different places to choose from. It was sometimes difficult to make a decision on where to go. Coming from the country, where normally you would have been lucky to get a single dance all night long, you now found yourself in places in Dublin where women out numbered the men by four or sometimes five to one.

The scene then was very different. The dance halls where Joe Dolan, Dickie Rock (spit on me, Dickie) were playing, were filled at eleven o'clock. Other big acts such as Big Tom, Ray Lynam, Philomna Begley, Susan McCann, Larry Cunningham, Gene Stuart, Margo would fill any place and they played every night of the week.

The trick at the time was to visit as many places as you could. One night, you could start out in one place in Parnell Square and soon after you might want to move around. You might get to go to three other places and then finish up in the same hall as where you started. The next best move you could make was to get to know the doorman. He would give you the nod to go inside for a quick look around. 'Who did you see?' was the standard question asked then. They were the good old times, an age when no drink or drugs were needed for you to enjoy yourself.

Admission into those dance halls then was about two shillings but you still had to watch your money as the pay was probably less than £20 per week. Your average night out would cost you less than £1 running around Parnell Square. Bed-sits then cost £3 or £4 per week, then traveling by bus to work, eating and maybe a few pounds sent home or put in the Post Office. Banks were above most workers that time.

At that time, phone calls cost a lot of money, which led to some enterprising people trying to use different tactics to overcome the cost of these calls. Guitar strings tied around the coin when it was dropped into the coin box and then pulled back out it would not work if you needed operator assistance. The best way around that was to get to know an operator from your socializing and then you'd be saving big time on the phone calls.

The ESB meter was another severe drain on the pocket. With electricity costing two shillings at the time, magnets were used to try and slow down the electricity meter from turning. It was no good using washers, although when they were tried, some worked but when the landlord used to open up the box, that was the end of that. The only thing I remember that actually worked was the 'two shilling ice coin'. Bottle tops were collected and filled with water. They were then put into the fridge and afterwards 'frozen coins' were made. Then, you put them into the meter and got your four units worth of electricity. However, it was important to place a heater near the meter in order to dry out the water that came from the melting ice.

The electricity was coming at the right price. I don't remember anyone been caught for the ice method but the practice died out when the 50p coin was introduced and new meters were installed.

Arriving in Dublin.

When you'd arrive in Dublin you would probably have stayed with someone you had known until such a time as you got your own bed-sitter or perhaps you may have managed to get someone else to look after you in the form of digs. At that time, there were only a few places known to have digs, one on the Southside and one on the Northside. The place on the Southside was run by a woman she had a couple of houses and it was there that you slept. For breakfast, you had to go to another place she had a few doors down the street.

Then, on the Northside, there was a place run by a man and wife team and they started out with six or seven men lodgers. After a few years, they had built up this number to about fifty with every part of the house converted over to take beds, the attic alone had about fifteen beds. This family business was well run with strict control, no foul language, no shouting or raised voices, no card playing during Mass time on a Sunday and no women was ever allowed inside the door.

Breakfast was served from 7.30am. until 9am. You were expected to get up for breakfast, whether you were working or not. If you did not get up in time, the food was left on the table. More often than not, there would be five to six breakfasts left on the table each morning uneaten. You were always called at 8am, even if you were not working until late that day, now, if you had to be working by 9am, you would be called at around 8.05am and told that it's getting late. 'It's going for nine, you'll be late,' so when you jumped up and got ready, you'd find that you had plenty of time.

When asked about this, the man of the house said once 'it's a minute after 8 am, it's going for nine and breakfast finishes at nine.' The Evening meals started at 5.30pm. If you were working late, it was kept for you. Every plate would be cleared, nothing left and no second helpings. When the plates were collected from the table, the only comment you'd have would be 'Just the right amount, just the right amount'. However, if truth be told, it was not always the right amount and a little more now and again would have been appreciated.

There was often grumblings about not having enough to eat but no one would complain. The cutlets served for the dinner had more bone than meat and one day, someone was leaving the digs and they were asked to comment or say something regarding the meat. He agreed to say something, now, the evening before his departure, we were all sitting around the dinner table, about twelve men and we all put the bones of the cutlets on the one plate. A huge pile of bones was presented to the man in charge of the dinner.

The man that was going away says 'Mr., can I say something to you regarding the dinner?' 'Go ahead' was the reply. 'My Father used to say, when you buy land, you buy stones, but Mr., when you buy meat, you buy bones'. 'Well, what's the inference' was his reply. None of us knew the meaning of the word 'inference' but it made no difference, the cutlet quality remained the same.

Jobs.

Most of the lads staying in the digs would have been building workers. There were a couple of builders or subcontractors staying with us as well and if you were a good worker and not wanting too much money, they would always be offering you a job. Some of the contractors told you in the interviews that 'if you do four times the work that I do on your first day and five times after that, then, you're my man'. If you were late for work, it was said that you had a great way of sleeping. If you over slept, you would be told that 'since you had to get up anyway, 7am. is just the same as 11am.'

I remember been asked one time, how much sleep I needed. I replied that eight hours would do me. This of course led to a lecture. 'Eight hours, you're the same value when you are asleep as when you're dead, no good for anything'. The lecture continued, 'If you live to be sixty (which seemed a be a long way off when you're in your twenties) and you sleep eight hours every night, then that's twenty years you were dead on this Earth'.

Eating, well that really was a mean habit for us. Breakfast and evening meal should have been enough. Stopping for a half hour at lunch time was a complete waste of time and on Saturday's, your day was shorter. Well, you finished up at around four or five instead of the regular six o'clock. It was highly recommended to you that no lunch break be taken. 'How could you be hungry on a Saturday when you have been eating all week'. That was one such comment that was widely used.

When you were looking for an increase in pay, well, that would have been real difficult since you would not know what to do with the extra money. 'All that extra money will ruin Ya" was another wise crack. It often happened that you would be out late the night before and you wouldn't be able to get up for work on time. You would be told that, whatever you had in mind, if you had not done it by ten, it was time to abandon that plan for that night. Oh, those were the good old days.

I remember one time that one of the workers lost his pay packet on the way home. I told the man who paid him that it was a terrible thing, 'loosing his pay'. The wise contractor was quick to respond, 'Well, sure he would have lost it by Sunday anyway.'

I hope that today, some of those contractors are still looking for staff because now-a-days they will have to have changed their ways in doing business. Now the young people are concerned only about two things, how much money am I getting and what time do I finish?

Also, starting time is when they get there!.

Working in Birmingham.

Going to England to work was a major step to take but the only one open to me at the time. There were all kinds of strikes all over Ireland, the cement strike and bank strike particularly affected the country. Going off to England was the only option I could take. I decided on going to Birmingham since I knew someone there that could help me out with lodgings and perhaps getting a job.

When I arrived in Birmingham, my first setback was when I was not able to make contacted with the person I was hoping to meet. After waiting a day and a night at the New Street Train Station, some changes in my plans had to be made. Eventually contact was made with that person and a place to stay was arranged and within a day or two, I had a job lined up as well. The £19 that I brought to England and had minded so well was getting smaller, but I wasn't too worried since I was soon starting work and money would be following soon after. Friday came and I was expected to get paid, however, this did not happen. I didn't even get the 'I will see you Sunday after Mass' treatment. Mass is hard to find over in Birmingham.

This was the first time in my life that I found out about having to work a week in advance. At this stage, my money had almost run out and was all gone by the following Monday. I had to borrow a few pounds from one of the lads in order to get by until that Friday. Friday being the payday, I was sure that everything would be all right. The pay packet came as a big shock to me, a check.

Since I had never gotten a check in my life and didn't know what to do with it, I had to ask around for instructions. 'Take the check to the bank to cash, however, you need to have an account open in order to cash the check.' I was told. On top of that this check was crossed which meant that it had to be lodged and I could only get the money out when the check had cleared. I had never heard of anything like this before.

All weekend long, I had no money, I hadn't eaten for days and I had no hope of getting any food over the weekend. The only person I knew was gone away for the weekend and that following Monday was a Holiday. I had no choice but to wait until the Tuesday. When Tuesday arrived, I was in fairly bad shape and the weakness was setting in. After about an hour working, I fell down and the English foreman was quickly on the scene. He asked me what had happened and when I told him the story of having no food for many days, he said 'Blyme, Blyme, come with me'. He took me to a local café and bought me breakfast. He then took me to the bank and opened up an account for me. He then gave me and advance on some money, a 'sub' as it was called and sent me home to recover.

It was a lovely gesture by a stranger and something that I would never forget. I left Birmingham about 6 months later and returned to Dublin. I was a much wiser man and at least, I had learned the hard way, what a crossed check was.

Driving.

When you are driving an old car, sometimes you are just waiting for it to break down. However driving the old Consul, it would be surprising at how long the model would keep running, it was often called 'the hearse' but call it what you liked, it was a great machine. They went forever and if you hit the ditch, the ditch moved. Afterwards, you drove through the ditch, found a gate and drove back onto the road again. There was none of your fiberglass panels back then. At those times, cars were made to last and had great stuff in them.

I remember when I bought my Consul for £53. I had it for about a year and a half and by the end of that time, I would describe the car as 'getting tired'. Around that time, I wanted to go to a dance which was about fifty miles away from me but I was not sure if the

Consul would make the trip or not. As it happened, I was in the middle of doing a deal with another man for a newer machine and in the deal, he was going to take my car and I was going to buy his. Now his would finish up costing me more since I would be giving him money with my car but that's the way it was.

Anyway, come time for me to test drive his car, I decided to take it for a good long test drive. I got into the car and off I went with two or three more passengers. Since I wanted to test her out good, I decided to give a trip over to the Dance Hall which was fifty miles away. We got there safe and well and the first car that was parked outside the dance hall was my own Consul. The other man was a Philomena Begley fan as well and decided to test my car out as well on a long trip. Both cars had made the trip there and back and as a result, the deal broke down. I held on to her for a while longer. I eventually sold it for £50 six months later. Back then, Cars did not lose their value as fast as they do now.

Racers In The 70's.

Crime in most parts of Ireland during the Sixties and Seventies was not a major problem. Topping the bill would be stuff like unlicensed dogs, no lights on bikes, so on and so forth. I remember there was an on going race that was causing some talk in the community. At the time, the proposed race was between a Honda 50 motorbike and the Ford Prefect car. The race was to be held near the local town and after about ten minutes into it, both racers had reached their top speed of about nineteen miles per hour. At that stage, both drivers were locked together and going flat out, no one would give an inch. This battle was going to prove whichever is faster, two wheels or four wheels.

The local Garda had been tipped off about this venture but since his transport was just a pedal cycle, he was not going to be in any position to catch them. The best he could do would be to conduct a follow up operation. He arrived at the culprits home and checked if the Honda was still hot from the race. His trip out to the house took ages and by the time he arrived, both engines were stone cold, no race conviction as ever secured.

Another crime that went unsolved in the area was the car with no driver. A local woman had complained many times to the local Garda about this car that used to pass her out when she was cycling. The car would blow the horn at her and apparently it had no driver. This fiasco went on for a long time. That would make you think back of the times that crowds used to turn out to watch moving statues around the country, watching for driverless cars should have drawn as many people.

Some time later, the Garda got a car for himself and this allowed for a major crackdown on crime. Now, I remember a time when a local farmer left the town to drive home. Now, he would not be paying much attention to driving, just minding his own business and hoping that everybody else would mind theirs. He motored along the road but he was followed by the Garda in the Car. The Farmer took a left turn, then a right turn and any other turn that was needed to get himself home. However, he had no indicator to speak of and he never looked in the mirror. He drove all the ways home, turning right towards the house and parked in the front.

The guard followed him into the yard and told him that he was behind him all the ways and that he never indicated or looked in his mirror. The Farmer replied, 'I've been living here in this same house for the last sixty years and you must be the only one who doesn't know that I lived here, I thought everybody knew I lived here!'

Driving In A Hurry.

When you are driving in a hurry in a car when you're young, you think that you are invincible. You believe that nothing can or will happen to you. This, of course is so wrong and has proved to be the downfall of many a young man. Driving fast is just one of many dangerous bad habits that you can develop. I suppose that I was no better or worse than most but I remember one night, I was in an unusually big hurry in order to get from Tuam to Roscommon. Unfortunately, I got caught behind a Morris Minor doing about 20mph just outside the town of Tuam. That same road would have been very narrow and proved to be very difficult to overtake somebody.

I stayed behind him for what seemed like forever, in actuality it was probably only about ten minutes but I just blew the horn to see would the driver ever even consider pulling in to let me get by. No bloody way, he had control and he was holding onto it. I blew the horn again and this time one of the occupants of the car turned around in the back seat and looked out the window, it was a calf. I eventually passed them out and with the speed I was doing, I was lucky not to have been involved in an accident.

A punishment for my mad driving, I learned a lesson that day that I should take my time, because, when I got into Roscommon, the man in the old Morris Minor with the calf was there before me. Although I was driving about three times faster, he obviously knew all the short cuts.

It's always a good policy to check the map, if you are not sure of where you are going. Slow and steady wins the race.

Water For Petrol.

Driving a car in the Seventies was, for most parts easy. There were not that many cars on the road and anyone with a car was in constant demand for a lift to the nearest town, shop, church or dances. Distance, when you had a car, was no object, a trip of forty or fifty miles didn't bother anybody. The price of petrol in the early seventies was not that expensive since the Arabs had not realized the full value of the oil. However the price shot up when they stopped supplies for a while and that created a panic. Since then, the price has only gone up and up.

I remember buying petrol one time at a country petrol station, it was a one pump, 200-gallon tank type of set up. After traveling about a mile down the road, the car stopped. I open up the bonnet, hoping and praying for a miracle that it might fix itself and take me to wherever I was going but no such luck.

Shortly afterwards, I was joined by a local man, who was enquiring from me what was the problem.

'Have you petrol in it, because them yokes need petrol to keep them going?' 'Yes', says I, 'I just got some back the road'. 'Check the petrol line and make sure the carburetor is getting the petrol' he says. I opened the clip and checked the fuel line. I then turned on the ignition and checked that the fuel was flowing. Everything looked fine but upon further inspection of the liquid in the fuel line, it did not smell like petrol, it was more like water and when we tasted it, water it was.

'He sold you water' the man said. 'On Me Solemn Oath, it's water, no doubt. Go back to him'. So I walked back to the station and told the man about what he had given me. 'Oh, we must be out of petrol again, the bottom off the tank holds water, that's probably what you got. Come back in a day or two and we'll have petrol again.'

In the meantime, I got some unscheduled exercise.

Windscreen Repair Service.

This service was designed for small repairs on glass and I cam across it at an auto show. It worked very well on small cracks (or what were called bullet cracks) that would occur when the windscreen is hit by a chip off the road. Car windscreens are made of two layers of glass, so what happens is that, when hit by a road chip the outer layers gets cracked but the inner layer remains perfect. The service offered was to remove the crack by filling in the offending hole with liquid glass.

The equipment that was needed to be bought cost a lot. It was more of a kind of franchise and if you did not buy the equipment from the dealer, you would not be supplied with the liquid glass. After some time, I managed to buy a used system with the promise that I would get the liquid glass whenever needed.

Anyway, when I took the equipment back to Ireland, it was then I found out that, only a small amount of windscreens would have been suitable for the repair with this system. The equipment needed for the Irish market was much less expensive, a brush to sweep it up and a small bag to put the shattered glass into. If you wanted to go hi-tech, a small vacuum cleaner would have done the job fine.

Clocks.

This particular idea was not to reinvent the clock but to put them into things that were all ready made. An example would be to insert a clock into blocks of Mahogany, Hurley sticks and the like. At that time, there were loads of pictures of Elvis, God, the Pope and Big Tom, and all begging out to have a clock attached to them. I had large post cards stuck onto a block of wood, then glazed over. It took me a while to find this glaze material but once I found out it's proper name, it was easy to get the stuff – it was called 'plastic coating'.

It worked well on most pictures but from time to time there would be a problem, some pictures would react to the coating and change the color. I remember one time when a picture of Elvis turning black and his guitar finished up looked like a cross between a hurley and a coffin lid, but not to worry, production continued despite any temporary setbacks. This plastic coating was also used on tabletops, counter tops and put to many more uses.

Mirrors.

This I expected to be a real winner, basically making mirrors in the shape of Ireland. After some attempts, it was decided that cutting out the shape of Ireland from mirror glass was not going to work that well. I finished up with pieces that looked more like the Caribbean Islands than Ireland.

Plan B was to get mirrored paint and apply it to wood that was already cut out in the shape of Ireland. Now, this particular paint was not something that you would find down at the local hardware store, there was no Internet available at that time, so everything had to be done without the click of the mouse. It took a lot of searching in magazines, making telephone calls and a huge amount of time was spent trying to get that information.

Eventually some progress was made and the mirror or silver paint was found. However, the cost was too much as one needed to spend at least three or four thousand pounds on it. That was the minimum amount that had to be bought from the supplier which I think was a method of helping keep the mirror business closed to small time operators.

In the meantime, I had a friend in the business and when I was telling him about my predicament, he told me about a material called 'Mirror Perspex'. That day was a happy one indeed. It didn't matter where in the world it was, I was going to get it. With this breakthrough, I started cutting out my shapes with a jigsaw and similar tools. At first, I was losing most of Kerry and some of Cork but when I used finer tool, things were shaping up nicely.

I got it to a stage where my mirrors were being cut out in the shape of Ireland and they looked very good. I sold a bunch of them at Irish festivals and some craft fairs. To this day, I still get the odd request for them. Now, that all the research and work has been done, there's no problem with supplying them.

The Lotto Dartboard.

'Just one more idea and I'll be making millions'. When the Lotto started up in Ireland, there was great excitement. Everybody was playing and there was loads of money spent. I was trying to figure out a way on how to get my hands on some of that money and I came up with the idea of the 'Lotto Dartboard'.

I was thinking that when picking the numbers, one had to have some sort of system and if you had a lotto dartboard, it's as good as system as any.
You can include the whole family in the fun and it seemed that this idea would go down a treat.

It's a pity that the lotto organization didn't start out with forty numbers. Trying to divide a dartboard up into thirty nine separate sections wasn't as easy as it would be, if it was forty. I used plenty of colors and the whole thing turned out very well. I was thinking to myself that this was fun and it was just what the world needed. I had grand notions of exporting to other countries since the lottery was played there too. All I was short was someone to market the product. The product itself was perfected by a cover that you'd put over the board, throw your darts and whatever numbers you hit on the board would be your lucky numbers!.

While I was planning what to do with my windfall of monies from the lotto dartboard sales, some Australian boyos were calculating out the odds of playing every combination of the thirty nine numbers and then placing those plays with the lotto organization. Unfortunately, for me, their plan worked out better than mine and they won a load of money in the four, five and six number drawings. Apparently, they had done the same in Australia some time before that.

As a result, the lotto scrapped the thirty nine number system and settled on the forty two number system thus putting myself and the other characters out of business.

The Reusable Matches.

The idea of the reusable match seemed to be a good one and I expected that everyone would be interested in such a product. Essentially what I had was a match built into in a steel case, not unlike a cigarette lighter. A flint would provide the spark and a wick that was threaded through the match would swing out and light up. At the base of the wick was a sponge soaked in lighter fuel.

The match worked fine but the customer did not take to it that well and soon they were all back using the regular matches.

The Clapper

Now when this contraption came out, it was supposed to do various things for you such as switch on your TV or your lights. All you had to do was sit down and clap your hands. I found that the only things that it could do was to alert people close by and get them to do the job that needed doing and it also keep your hands warm while trying to get the bloody thing to work in the first place.

Whatever it's intended use still remains a mystery to this day.

The Perfect Mouse Trap.

The perfect mousetrap was next. It's a well-known fact what the world needs the perfect mousetrap and I thought that I had found it. It was an electronic device that the theory was that you just plugged it in and the mice simply left the building. Where did they go? Over to the next house. The device looked good, the house owner was happy that the mice would finally be leaving. He was looking forward to a mouse free, happy house.

A mouse can be pretty frightening to some people in much the same way as a cat can be frightening to the mouse. Someone should tell the mice that cats now-a-days are used to much better quality meals and for most parts are not interested in mice as an alternative source of energy. This new electronic mouse trap would be used to terrorize every mouse and would be needed worldwide. The plan was simple. Find out where the mice were, go to that house and sell the mouse trap to that owner. Then wait a day or two and go to the house that that mouse moved to and sell that owner another trap. A piece of cake for the seller, it was a sure bet and we were all going to be happy.

However, whatever signal the mouse trap was supposed to send out to frighten the mouse, must have gotten mixed up with something else. Wherever the trap was laid, the mice were extremely happy and comfortable. They all stayed where they were and you may as well have used the clapper instead by throwing it at them in order to make them move.

Who knows, maybe the electronic mouse trap would have worked better as a clapper on the TV and the lights and vice versa.

The Eye Spy.

I've seen a new idea in the early Seventies, it was a small plastic tube with what appeared like a plastic lens attached at one end. I bought hundreds of them when I should have only bought maybe six since I just wanted to see how they worked. This new business venture of mine was called 'safety service'. My plan was to make every home safer. When the doorbell rang, you'd just go to the door and look out through this device before you opened it, it was supposed to be an amazing security upgrade at your own door.

Now the plan was to set up, sell and install these amazing security systems. After a few installations and a couple of doors with holes in them, it became obvious that these devices weren't as good as they were let on to be. In fact, you'd see more if you looked out through the hole that was made on the door in the first place, without the device being installed. The eye spy was even supposed to let you see around corners. Unfortunately, it did not do what it was supposed to do.

The question now was, how was I going to get rid of the hundreds that I had bought? I had to come up with Plan B which was to advertise them in the evening papers, alas, there was no response. When I advertised them on the Sunday papers, I only got one reply from a prison who said they were looking for extra security. They were going to have it with this piece of plastic, no doubt. The next step was to sell them to students who would go door to door selling them during the summer holiday. It was going to be their first stepping-stone to becoming millionaires.

My sales pitch was simple, buy twenty and that amount would get you started in business. I was able to sell most of them to the students and it was a great experience for them to get started in the real world.

Handball.

In the Sixties, there was not much happening in the line of sports. Kicking a football would be as much as you can do. However, if you were lucky enough to live close to a handball alley, you would have played there in the evenings. In this sport, you were not given much encouragement by the players that were already established. Sunday was the main day and all day long the older players took over the place. You would never be able to get a game, it was a long apprenticeship and either darkness or thirst was the only thing that would stop the playing for the other players. Only those who were really interested would have persevered and finally be inducted into the exclusive club of handball.

At that time, all the handball alleys were outdoors, there would have been anything from one wall to four walls and they were all called handball alleys. Handball was called the 'life long' game which was even played by men that were into their sixties or older.

After the regulars played among themselves, they might allow some younger players join in and have them do all the running while they waited for the ball to come. All the skilled players knew how to tire out the younger players and to make things worse, all the refereeing was done by the players themselves so the younger players were always at a disadvantage.

The dialogue from the refereeing was constant. It was long, it was short, it was this, it was that, it never stopped. When it got close to the finish, they had what was called a 'set'. This kicked in three or four aces from the end, if the two sets of players were anyway even and there was a chance the game might finish and more players would be able to get a game. Some players used to start the games over and over and sets could keep the game going for the whole day. What we had to do was keep waiting and hoping that the thirst will set in before the darkness. That meant that someone else would be able to get a game.

The best game of all was singles but that was not played that much. Doubles and trebles were the most popular and the winners of the game usually stayed on playing, taking on two or three other challenging players. The champion would stay there playing all day and it would take something like having to go home and milk the cows to make them finish the game of the day. On some outdoor alleys, a back wall was built which meant the loss of some players. The shock of a ball coming back from behind was just too much of a change for them.

Worse was to come when roof and lights were added which was great for the 60x30 alleys. Then someone found out about the handball popularity in USA and that they were playing it in a smaller court size of 40x20. So of course, anything that was been done in USA was sure to be better than Ireland and as a result, the 40x20 was introduced as a new game.

A handball court with a glass back wall was used and you could also use the ceiling as part of the playing area. A new blue colored ball which was as hard as a stone was used. You then wore leather gloves to save your hands and you wore special goggles for your eyes, however your body was still at risk from this round blue bullet.

The new craze, 40x20 handball, anybody could play it. This was a game that could be played by Grannies. The courts came complete with changing rooms and showers. New handball players were coming on line and some were equipped with tennis rackets. These were the new breed of handball players and more and more players were coming out in their droves, playing this sport.

Then a few ladies joined and the sport quickly became the new 'exercise' sport. Another contributor to this game's demise was that some of the 60x30 players never took to the 40x20 game. They either formed small pockets of resistant or else retired to the local pub and started playing pool. The 60x30 has since made a small come back but the biggest mistake was that they build so many small 40x20 alleys in most counties in Ireland. We now have more alleys than players.

A county could have up to twenty handball alleys and maybe six or eight players. A long time hand ball player that was involved in the game's administration told me this happened everywhere in Ireland.

A huge local effort was involved and a new court would be ready for the official opening. The top players from around the country would be invited and they always came to put on an exhibition. The women would be there too with the tea and sandwiches. The invited players would be given some trophy for winning or at least taking part. They often gave the trophy away to some young player, which was very nice of them. When the top players then left, the local players took over, they were dressed in Wellingtons or boots and some of them came with their tennis rackets. This was the grass roots of the 40x20 hand ball movement.

Handball would have been better served if the 60x30 alleys had been built and developed rather than copying the 40x20 from another part of the world. After all it was an Irish game, so why not let them follow us. Now-a-days, only a few players are still playing the old game of 60x30 and a lot of the big alleys have been knocked down. The tidy towns committees were not big handball fans so, they decided that a lot of the handball alleys were to be demolished. Their thinking was, flatten the alleys and put a few barrels with flowers in that space. That then would improve their chances in the tidy towns competition.

I myself played handball for many years and it is a great game. The rewards was in the playing and we traveled the country. No expenses were ever provided nor expected. Win or lose did not matter to us, it was just the love of the game made you a winner all the time.

The Vending Machines.

The cigarette vending machine business seemed to be just right. All you had to do was fill the machine up and collect the money. Well, that was the theory but unfortunately there was not enough money to be made out of them. The way you got into this business was that you bought some machines and sited them yourself or else you bought a cigarette round that usually went at a big price. The machines were costing £40 or less to buy, then they were sited and when sold the price often reached £400 per machine in lots of ten.

They were sold as a unique business and going concern. For ten to twelve hours work per week, you'd net £150 - £200 profit. The job would suit a retired person but you needed loads of money because the investment was definitely for the long term. A good cigarette vending machines round would make some money for you especially if you had a few good bars with two machines. Fill them twice a week then there was possibility of making something.

Unfortunately, there were some cowboys who were in it for the fast buck. The plan here was to put machines anywhere and everywhere, for example, outside petrol stations. These machines usually disappeared off the wall after a couple of weeks. When it came to the Night clubs, where you would sell less than ten packets a week and have four machines in each location, well, that was a complete waste of time and money for anyone who bought such a round.

The people selling the machines for this unique business did not care, just put the machines in and sell them off as a business. I've seen many people loose a lot of money in cigarette vending. I saw a man once who came to Dublin from the country and he had a bucket of money. It looked like that the bucket was buried underground because there was clay on top of the stones and the money was hidden under the stones. There was about £3000 of the old money in there and some of it was of the old pound shillings and pence. It did not matter too much to the sales team, anything that looked like money, they took it and they were able to find use for it. The person with the bucket of money bought seven sited machines in two nightclubs and his profits was probably about £20 for the seven machines per week.

After a few weeks the person that bought them would realize that there was very little coming out of this unique business. When he asked for the machines to be re-sited or re-sold, the sales team would be very happy because they would sell them on again to some other sucker. In the meantime, the man with the bucket of money (and many more like him) would be left waiting for their money. All types of different charges would be made and eventually no money would be left. All gone and nothing to show for it.

There were many people caught in that scam. However, the man with the bucket of money did not like what had happening to him, he arrived back one day with a shotgun and that was the end of that joke. I can tell you, he got some of his money back, but not all of it.

Even with things were going well, it was hard to make any serious money. You always had people looking for free cigarettes. They were looking for samples, if a new brand was coming on the market. The cigarette manufacturer would always send a few hundred new branded cigarettes and you'd put them into the machine. However, those cigarettes would never sell and you'd eventually have to take them out again. To make things worse, you'd get an invoice for them, maybe a year later.

Another setback to the business would have been when there was a price increase, like a budget increase. The machines had to be converted over to accommodate the new price and this could cost £20 to £30 per machine, and that was more money that was difficult to recover.

As most of the machines were mechanical, it was easy to use dud coins. The old 50p coin was easily made when the old penny was adapted by simply cutting one or two corners off it and then it passed as 50p piece. I remember going into a dance hall one time and seeing two columns of cigarettes in the machine gone, only to realize that when I opened it, I found twenty old pennies in each column. Another coin was the lead 50p which was easily made in any workshop where there were cutters.

Then you had the joker that bought a packet of cigarettes, removed the packet and replaced it with an empty packet. That meant that the next person to buy a packet would have gotten an empty packet. It was great fun, no doubt, to the joker. Usually before a budget, there would be a shortage of cigarettes that would have been made by the manufacturer. It was supposed to curtail stockpiling. You would be doing well to have enough money to buy what you needed and not to mind stockpiling.

The big increase would happen and then you had all the cigarettes you wanted, the only thing was that the machines would still need to be converted. As a result, there was always going to be a couple of days of waiting to get machines changed over to the new price. Then you had people complaining there were no cigarettes available before the increase and that the operator was making a fortune. At some of the places where you had machines, they wanted the keys so as they would not be short of change. 'More commission' someone said, 'they would give another 1% more, can you give us more brands?' Others were complaining, 'someone looked for this brand, can you put that in?' and then whoever looked for it, must have given up smoking or else went off to Australia.

I once bought 10 machines in England for £200. They were four column machines and I thought that I would fit them in as an extra machine in a location maybe to put some of the once off lines beside a six column machine. They had the 50p columns but I thought that I would convert them over to whatever. After further examination, I found out that they could not be converted. The search was now on for something to sell for 50p and try and make some money.

After much searching, I decided I would sell ladies tights. So the next job was to site these machines in dance halls, nurses homes and hospitals. I thought these would be good sites and installed them there. I bought the tights, put them into the vending machines and waited and waited. Not one box was sold. I think that, from that time on, women went off tights and I had a lot of stock for a long time.

Audio Cassette Machines.

Cassette machine were supposed to be the new entertainment for restaurants and pubs in the Seventies. They would have been regarded as being up-market in comparison to juke boxes. However, when they first came out, they only had a selection of 10 cassettes, so you just couldn't satisfy everyone. You had the likes of Neil Diamond, Roy Orbison and James Last. They were the big names then, all very sensible artists and you had no worries about the rappers we have now in those times.

The cassette machine was intended for the mature listener, easy listening while dining, a good idea but a slow moneymaker.

Video Games.

When the video games appeared on the scene, they were a very simple job. The game mostly played was a wall that you would knock the bricks out of and build them then on the other side. It was a simple game by today's standard, there was no blood or brains being knocked out. As time went by, the games got more exciting but not by much.

Bumper Pool Tables.

Pool was one of the better games people played. The tables needed very little maintenance and a steady income was had by almost everyone. I tried to introduce a new game into Ireland at one time. It was called 'bumper pool'. This was a game that was played in the USA and Canada and was very popular there. The tables looked similar to the pool tables except that they had two pockets, one at each end.

Now the shipping of the tables from the USA to Ireland would have been too expensive so the alternative available to me would be to get the accessories in the USA and add them then to the pool tables in Ireland. It was not that easy to get the parts and the bumpers proved very difficult to obtain. Twelve of them were needed for each table. There were eight bumpers set up in the form of a cross in the middle of the table,. At each end there were two more with one at each side of the pocket. The object of the game was that you could not put the ball direct into the pocket, you had to bounce it off a bumper in the middle of the table.

There were ten balls used in the game in total, five for each player and you started off at the end of the table. You then had to put them into the pocket at the other end. I converted over some of the pool tables and installed them in different places, however, the game lasted too long and although it was a good game, it was another slow money taker.

The Roller Skates.

The roller skate craze started in the early eighties and they were difficult to find. The only ones available were those that you could buy overseas in the USA and later in Britain. I placed a small advert in an evening paper to see if there would be any response. It turned out that there was a good response and since Christmas was coming and roller skates were at the top of the list item for gifts. I used to go to London with two suitcases and fill them with skates. I used to buy about thirty pairs of skates at a time. You must remember that, at that time, there were no wheels on the suitcases, so it was important to have a strong pair of arms.

I did that trip a few times but I was always behind on my orders. I then started to take a car over to England and fill it up with skates and drive back through the North. However, the cost of taking a car back through Holyhead was about four times more expensive than traveling through "Larne" and keeping the cost down was always the name of the game.

That year, the supply of skates was a long way short of demand and even after Christmas there was still a demand. By the following Christmas, the supply had improved and skates were much more readily available.

My next move was to start operating some roller discos. Armed with about two hundred and fifty pairs of skates, I rented a hall, played some music and started skating discos. I had two sessions a night playing in different venues, Friday, Saturday and Sunday from six to eight for the under fifteens and then 8.30 to 11.30 for the rest, anybody and everybody turned up.

Those discos were big. I can tell you that every pair of skates were used and no one would be complaining about the size, they made them fit somehow and they put them on and started skating.

When the music stopped and the two hundred and fifty pairs of skates were dumped at the door, you then loaded the skates into the back of the Hiace van and drove home.

To this day, the smell of the skates its still with me, its everlasting. You do the same thing the next night, making a lot of young people happy but there would be always a few who'd finish up with sore ankles and bruised bodies from falling down on the ground. Falling, would be something you should try to avoiding because there would be a stampede going around the floor. Staying upright on your feet, would be the slogan for survival.

Concerts.

In the early Eighties, everything seemed to be going on in Dublin. You'd have the celebrity act that you'd see on TV but who had never come down the country. So giving them the opportunity to perform outside Dublin seemed to me to be a good idea, however they didn't seem too anxious to do a bit of traveling. Traveling outside the postal code of Dublin was not usually done, especially at the weekends.

However, the ones that did venture outside the golden circle wanted to be paid very well, probably twice amount they would be getting in Dublin. I suppose, it was a kind of disturbance money. Some of the acts realized at an early stage that they were not as popular as they thought they were down the country. It happened that the amount of people that turning up at some of the venues was not even enough to pay the VAT on the agreed price, not to mind the fee.

I remember an act that booked for £1000, but after a TV appearance their fee quickly jumped to £3000. It was lucky for everyone concerned that a large snow storm came and of course, you could not expect the stars to travel in that kind of weather. By the time the snow melted common sense had set in and no concert took place thus avoiding a lot of embarrassment.

At one time, a big act arrived down an hour or two before the concert was to begin so they set up their gear and put their suits in the dressing room and went to the local pub. Security in the Eighties would not have been very high at those venues and two of the local jokers decided to dress up in the band's outfits. They were apprehended, with instruments in hand, while they were warming up before getting onto the stage. Their version of 'The Irish Rover' had to wait for another night.

Another famous act had their fee set at £4000, and there's a lot of collecting even today in £4000, and after a great performance the time of reckoning soon arrived. Now, most of the money had already been collected on tickets that had been sold before the show. The first complaint the Band had was the running of a raffle. They announced, 'We are not a parochial hall act, we have played all over the world and there should not be a raffle held where we play'. Now the best you could hope for, in order to have any money out of a concert like that, would be whatever you got from having the raffle. The takings on the night were a little short of what was needed, so when paying the band, we had to borrow some money from the raffle. All of a sudden, the parochial hall money was ok!.

Even that was not enough. When we complained we were making no money out of the concert, the band said 'what about the money from the mineral bar. Didn't you get money there?' I suppose we should have been happy with that.

Pitch And Putt.

A pitch and putt course seemed an easy way of making some money, cut the grass and then collect for the clubs. There were ten acres of land for lease in North County Dublin and it seemed to be the ideal position for a course. This land itself had not been used for anything for many years. An old man living across the road said that the last crop to grow there were potatoes and that they only grew the size of marbles. That was sometime after the Second World War and probably the crop of potatoes before that was grown during the potato Famine.

You would think growing grass should be easy. However, it's not that easy when you want it to grow, first, you have to get rid of the long useless grass that's there already. The next move was to cultivate and seed the ground. All this effort was costing money but I was sure that the return would have been great. After months of waiting for grass to grow and indeed, very little of it was growing, it was decided to go ahead with stage two of the development of the course.

Now, what stands out most at any pitch and putt course is the beautiful greens but since I was going to be short of grass on this course, something else was needed for it to stand out and look like a pitch and putt course. I decided that bunkers would do the job. A friend of mine with a JCB was told to dig some bunkers on the course and since neither of us would have the Greg Norman design potential, there was no set measurements for the bunkers. When they were dug, you could easily hide armored tanks in them or with a little more work, they could be converted into caves.

I was still waiting for the grass to grow and at this stage, the best part of two years had passed since work started, this venture was fast running out of time and enthusiasm. One last desperate effort was made to save this enterprise and that was when an expert in agriculture was hired. Now, it would have been better if the advice had been sought two years prio or even if I listened to the man across the road who said that nothing ever grew in that field.

The agriculture expert said that with the amount of seed that was bought for that field it must have been used in another field in the next county, for all there was to show. In the meantime, while still waiting for the lush greens to develop, a new opportunity arose.

The Pope was coming to Ireland and everyone was trying to figure out how to make money out of this once in a lifetime opportunity. The ten-acre field that I had would have made an ideal car park, as a huge amount of traffic was expected to descend on Dublin from the North Side. However, all kinds of restrictions were in operation regarding traffic and no traffic was allowed to drive through the City except those with special permits. Car parking facilities was regarded as a commercial venture and therefore, no permit would have been issued.

Alternative arrangements were then made to stay in the North Side and to cater for the early morning rush of cars, I had a few hours sleep in my car at the new car park. An early start was the order of the day. At 4am, I decided, it was time to open up. Another man who was helping me out on the day drove about seventy miles to the car park. At 4.05am, the first car arrived. The driver of the car wanted to park near the entrance so that he would not be blocked in by other cars. The first £1 was gained, we were up and running at long last, the ten acres was finally going to give a return for all of the hard work that had been put into it.

The original estimate of 600 cars looked like it could be met and I remember that if it got overcrowded, the bunkers could be turned into underground car parking. Everything was now ready and all we had to do was just wait. At 4.05am the first car, then came 5.05, 6.05, 7.05, 8.05, 9.05 and 10.05 and there was still only one car. It was then decided to abandon this plan and head off for the Phoenix Park and join the million that was there on that glorious day. At the end of the day, it was decided that there was one last opportunity left.

Deck chairs, everyone had them going there but on the way out, they were looking for someplace to get rid of them. Fortunately, I was there to take them and after collecting 300 chairs, I put them into the Hiace and headed straight for Knock and Galway. The great deck chair sale had started and some of the projected income was thankfully recovered.

I was wondering where all the cars we expected to be in the pitch and putt course went and I came to the conclusion that they stayed at home. Only a small amount of the expected crowd from the North came to the Phoenix Park because the Pope was also visiting Drogheda later in the week and many people waited and went to that event.

It has been said many times, 'if you don't try, you cannot win'. Another wise saying is, 'the man that never made a mistake, never made anything', however, the man that makes too many mistakes, makes nothing either.

Bath Resurfacing.

Bath resurfacing was a new service that came on the scene in Ireland more than twenty years ago. I first saw it done in the USA and thought that this would work in Ireland. Thinking that with nobody else but yourself doing it, how could you go wrong. I went to the resurfacing academy headquarters were I was accepted in up state New York. I was there for two days being shown how the system worked. There was also some brainwashing on how successful you were going to be after the two days of training. I was ready to take on the bath resurfacing franchise.

I would become a bath doctor once I had paid over $200,000 or I could have got the master franchise for Ireland, where I could sell off area franchises myself for about $2 million. It was not the sort of money that I had in mind but I had seen how the system worked, so I reckoned I could do it by myself and that I did.

I returned to Ireland and put an advert in the paper to see if I would get any response. Fortunately, the response was good and it was time to get the business up and running. I went looking for a ceramic paint and I found it after the long search. This particular paint was available in any color as long as it was white. I then bought a big air compressor and some top quality spray equipment. Money was no object since I had just saved $200,000 on not buying the franchise.

Next was the cleaning fluid. This proved hard to get and also there was some restrictions in buying it. Hydro fluoride acid is very dangerous and that was the chemical needed to clean the baths. Anyway, I got going on the work, I probably did not comply with all the health and safety regulations since after a while I noticed some burns and blisters appeared on my hand and face. I needed to start taking care of myself and but I soldiered on.

The technical word for the cleaning of the bath surface was etching. This would then leave the bath prepared for spraying. I was thinking that spraying with all this good equipment was going to be a piece of cake, or was it. My big compressor was too big for most houses and you would need to plug it into the national electricity grid to get it started. A smaller compressor worked much better.

Most of the baths that were to be sprayed were removed from the bathroom as the room was being re-modeled. This made it easy as I didn't have to cover up everything else in the room to save it from been accidentally sprayed. The system now seemed to be going well, the spraying equipment was much better and the spraying itself looked easy. You needed to have some idea of what you were doing or else you'd finish up with a few tram lines that otherwise you might not want to have.

Any color you liked, as long as it was white. Next came an order that required an immediate expansion of the operation. This person needed her toilet, hand basin and bath to be resurfaced. Not a problem, the confidence was high, however, there was a small problem with the color. It was not white that she was looking for but blue. Now, blue ceramic paint was not available and after a long unsuccessful search, I decided to use a blue enamel paint and just spray it on the surfaces.

Now this would be something new, it would have been first spray job indoors and maybe a new beginning in paint technology. Well, some changes were being made in the bathroom that were not entirely intended. Some of the spray paint was getting onto places that it should not be going and the bathroom was turning out more blue than expected. The new paint was not working as well as the white ceramic but I soldiered on. Some designs were appearing that were not intended, tram lines and waves and those were not included in the price.

Included in the American franchise price was a large heater. This was used to help in the drying of the paint, I think the term they called it was baking. Anyway, I did not have this dryer but I used a hair dryer instead which worked almost as good. I got the job completed and left the usual instructions to not use the bath for 48 hours, to make sure that the paint would be dry.

Well after the day or two had passed, the people of the house wanted to have a bath. A draw must have been made to see who would be first in the new bath and of course the woman of the house got the nomination.

As she sat in the bath, she could see a lot more blue than was needed. Bits of spray were all over the place but there was a bigger shock in store for her.

When she stepped out of the bath, her legs and rear end were colored blue. Unfortunately, the paint had not dried properly so now you had a half blue woman and a half blue bath. The bathroom was eventually returned to the white color.

Football & Hurling All-Ireland Key-Rings.

The All-Ireland Hurling and Football games were exciting times for most counties, especially when they got to the finals and I was thinking to myself that it would be nice to have a key ring of your favorite team. I then started making key rings for the hurling and football finals in 1989. In that year, Tipperary won the hurling and Cork won the football. To make it, I would get a team picture and reduce it in size and put it into a blank key ring with a photo of Croke Park on the back.

They were a big hit and to this day still are. Nobody else has done this kind of souvenir and now and again there might be a complaint that they are too big, I'd just say 'just get bigger pockets'. These All-Ireland winning team key rings have gone all over the world. Some people that buy them often say 'I am sending this to Australia, USA or to a friend, relative, son or daughter. Now, I have people coming back to me saying, 'I got this 10 years ago from you'. 'Well, in that case' says I, 'Maybe you would like one from the 21st century'.

Getting the key rings ready for the final was no problem but getting them ready with the score on them for the homecoming can be a rush. Cork and Kerry are a long way from Croke Park and you have to be in those places a few hours before the team arrives. That meant that production has to proceed with a lot of speed even as you were traveling to the home coming. I remember putting key rings together while I was stopped at the traffic lights at the dreaded Red Cow Roundabout.

In fact, lots of key rings have been put together while I was stopped in traffic, no time was to be wasted because you needed to have those key rings ready because there was only a time period of one to two days of selling while the excitement is there and then it would be all over.

I remember a few years ago, when Kerry won the All-Ireland and I was in Killarney for the home coming. At 9.30 on a Monday night, no one was on the street to greet the team. At

10pm, a tractor and trailer went to the end of the street and dropped off the trailer. A few chairs were put on the trailer and a couple of musicians started to play at around 10.30, shortly afterwards, that the team arrived and about 500 people turned up to meet them instead of the over 20,000 that were expected.

Now, that's a huge difference when you think of the memorable nights that I have attended down through the years. Clare in 1995, what a turn out, we had Wexford, Donegal, Galway, Tipperary, Armagh, Tyrone and Cork where I saw 30 or 40,000 people turning up for the homecoming.

Gold and Silver Key Rings.

I also made other key rings. I bought £5 worth of old pennies. Now, they were the pennies and half pennies that were in circulation before the decimalization came about in the early 70's or around that time. Then, there were 240 pennies in one pound and you would certainly need to have good pockets to carry them around.

These 1200 old pennies that I had would have needed some brightening up so I decided that I would like to plate them Gold and silver. Well, for a start, I was going to color them gold and silver, however, the standard that I was looking for meant that I had to get someone to plate them properly. After the usual long search, I found a company that sprayed handles for coffins and they said that they would do the job. All, I had to do to get the coins ready was to put them on wire hangers so that they're ready for spraying.

That meant that all the pennies had to be drilled, one at a time and this took a fairly long time to do but the completed job was well done in both the gold and silver. Over 1000 people are now the proud owners of the old gold and silver pennies with key rings attached. They've got to be a collector's item by now.

Paper Library.

This project was expected to fill those times that, if you were on your well-deserved holidays at the seaside and when the weather was not suitable for the beach, you could visit the paper museum. It was going to let you go back to the year 1900 or before and feature every major news story that was covered from around the world. Of course, it would also include the report from the papers of the day of every All-Ireland Final Football and Hurling from the start of the GAA founding.

This was going to be a must for everyone and with time to spare, many hours and days were spent in Dublin going through the papers from the past, selecting major stories and getting copies of the stories. It was decided that there should be a light hearted side to the stories too, after all, most of the news would have been of a serious nature, such as earthquakes, wars, plane crashes, and the like.

So I was thinking, why not get some papers with weird and wonderful content. I mean, you need look no further than the National Enquirer or similar papers for the wild and extraordinary news. Some of those papers are printed in Florida so needless to say, Florida was my next stop. After spending about two week there, going through the archives, I managed to get a couple a hundred of wild and weird stories put together.

Unfortunately, at that time, a problem arose at the national paper archive in Dublin. A dispute over upgrading their system which took many months, if not years to be sorted out, needless to say, in the meantime, other things came on line and by the time the paper archives had sorted out, I had moved on to other thinks.

Seaside Games Of Skill.

There are many games out there where you test your skill. I suppose the lotto could be classed as a game of skill, that is of course, if you pick the right numbers. The games of skill that I know of are usually found at the seaside resorts and they are operated under the heading 'games of skill'. Now, games of skill are completely different from games of chance which would be games designed to extract money from you as painlessly as possible.

The skill part is pitting your skill against the operator's skill and for most part, it's no contest. I remember once, having a visit from the local law enforcement agency. They were on a mission to clean up the places operating gaming machines that were paying out too much money. He asked me to show him the skill in these games which included dart games, rifle range games, derby racer and many more. I explained what had to be done to participate in these games but he was insisting they were all games of chance.

Some of the games, like the derby racer, has a winner every time and it is usually won by the most skilful player. So from that point of view, that's not illegal, it's your skill that wins the game. After a lot more talk, it was time for them to go. The seeds of doubt were planted and I was getting the benefit of the doubt. As he walked away, his parting shot was 'Games of Skill'. Skill alright buts it's you that has the skill, skill to take money from people. Most of the games there are for fun and no one is going to lose a big amount of money, it's not Las Vegas we're talking about.

You play if you want and no one forces you. You can sit down at the derby racer and roll the ball into the holes. Your horse moves along and whoever is the most accurate, wins. They then get a prize and go away and there's no major crime committed by anyone.

However, other games might need a little more skill, for example, darts. In this game, you throw the darts at the board in order to reach a certain number. According to some dart players, the odds are stacked against you. They'd complain that the darts are too light or too heavy or that the board is not at the right height. Often you'd hear, 'the distance you are standing is not the right distance, can I use my own darts?' 'I won this and that before, everything is set against you here'. Do they not realize that the good dart players often don't play well, away from home.

The Rifle Range.

Now this is one of the games that the most suspicion is placed opon. People referring to the rifles would be enquiring from me 'what do you do with them to put them off'. I usually tell them that I dance on them every hour and that helps to put the aim out. The truth is, there's no need to ever do anything and anyway, there's nothing you can do. Bend the barrel!. 99% of the people using the guns, would never have held a gun in their hands before. However, they still think that the first time they shoot the gun, that they'd be as good as James Earl Ray.

Here's another well worn question. I'd hear, 'has anyone ever done it, it's impossible'. It's not impossible but to some, getting the perfect score is. They'd claim 'I used to shoot rabbits from 30 yards, 50 years ago or was it 50 yards, thirty years ago with a shotgun'. That was using different equipment and maybe different eyes.

I know that Spec savers future is looking good.

The Cycle Race.

Another game I had, was called after the 'Tour de France' and it was a huge attraction. Myself and the best man that I have ever met, built it together. Patsy O'Connor, he could literally do anything. I would have ideas on many things and when I would discuss them with Patsy, the answer I always heard was 'I don't see why it would not work'. He was always positive and I never heard the words 'it won't work' from him.

The race consisted of 18 bicycles lined up together. The rear wheels were raised a couple of inches off the ground by a frame which allowing the rear wheels to spin. The 18 riders would all start the race together and their peddling would move a small cycle and rider on a track. Whoever cycled the fastest, would be the winner.

The sight of 18 cyclists going flat out was a great sight to see and always attracted a huge crowd of people. The only problem was, most people only went on the cycle race only the one time. Since it could have been 20 years since they were last on a bike, the legs might not be the same.

However, luck was on every rider's side because when they got off their bike, there was a pub, Kilorans, right beside them, so whatever energy that was lost during the race was quickly restored.

The Cyclomobiles.

Cyclomobiles were an attraction in many places down through the years. These were four-wheel cycles complete with a canopy on top to help keep you from getting sun burned but in Ireland it was more often used to help to keep the rain off the people riding the cycles. Two or three people could cycle on them at a time, well, that was what was intended but they were often turned into mini buses with people hanging out of them in the back and front. With the Mother, Father, two kids and often the granny and granddad all riding together, I decided to make the cycles bigger and put more seats and more pedals in them.

I came up with two rows of seats and have four people pedaling.
The cycles when used leisurely, were enjoyable and no danger to anyone. However, when you think of the speed that could be reached, with four people peddling and they all tanked up with drink, you'd sometimes hear them roar, 'get out of the way, juggernaut coming'.

As a result, the sight of the family out enjoying their holiday on those cyclomobiles is no longer seen because the high cost of public liability insurance put an end of them.

The Great Race.

This new game was meant to be played by up to twelve people and each person had there own replica sports car like a Ferrari, Lotus, Lamborghini, Mini Cooper and so on. All the cars were running on a track and this track was constructed on a large trailer in order to make it mobile. That meant it could be taken to different events and venues around the country.

The set up was that each player sat at a desk and there were three players to each desk. They each had a gear stick and had to change gears only when there was a green light signal. There were four gear changes 1st., 2nd., 3rd., and 4th. and you could only change gears when you got the green light. The green lights appeared only by careful driving and needless to say, those drivers were few and far between. After a long time working on it and getting it up and running properly, it was booked into a venue in Dublin.

Here, we were going to have it's maiden voyage and unfortunately, like the Titanic, the end result was the same. The cars were remote controlled and unfortunately, no one realized this but the radio frequency used in the controls was the same as that used by the ambulances in their communications. So whenever an ambulance passed, the cars took on a mind of their own and sometimes tried to follow them. This was Ireland's answer to Ambulance Chasers.

Unfortunately, the great race never reached it's full speed and potential in that format but a few years later, a new updated version was completed and it worked very well. The new system worked without any remote control

Games At The Seaside.

The punch ball machine was a simple test of strength. Those machines have been around a long time and all you had to do was put a coin in and you punch the soft ball. It was not very difficult and you would think that it would be fairly safe, once there was no head or anything like that near the ball. Sometimes, a strong man would not be satisfied with just punching the ball so he'd attempt to kick it. However, the height of the ball was too high and anyone who tried to kick it sometimes finished up with injuries.

One day, this drunk comes along, he was so drunk that he could not find the slot to put the money in. To make things simple for himself, he just drew out and punched the machine where you put the money in. I do not need to remind you that this is not a very soft part of the machine and he ended up with a sprained wrist.

He sued for injuries to his wrist. In Court, I tried to explain to the Judge the workings of the punching ball and this took a long time. This Judge mustn't have been let out too often because he did not understand or perhaps he did not want to understand what was going on. I explained that it was a vending machine and like any other vending machines, you put money into it and this one would let you test your strength.

The Judge said that once the machine takes the money, the owner or operator has the responsibility towards the person using it and if necessary, should provide that person with instruction on how to use it. He also claimed that the owner/operator should also act as security and not allow people to use the machine if they were under the influence of drink.

He was awarded something for the pain and suffering and that was the last punch thrown in that operation.

Selling Gold & Posters.

The summer season was always a good time to try and sell stuff. Everyone was out there peddling something or another, so I was thinking, what could be easier to sell than Gold earrings, chains and watches. I had the earrings for sale at 50p each and they were costing me the staggering price of 2 or 3 pence per pair or 6 pence, boxed. The question I was asked all day long was, 'is it real gold?' 'Yes, it is real gold' would be my reply', They'd come back 'is it guaranteed?' 'Yes', says I, 'guaranteed, when it goes black, it stays black'. The story was the same with the chains.

There was a man beside the gold stall and he was selling quality watches, they were guaranteed to go wherever your took them. From time to time, you get the smart man, you know, the one that knows it all and he would be looking for the best watch. 'What have you in Rolex?', Oh, said the seller, 'I have a special edition Rolex intended for people just like you.'

The name on the face of the watch was slightly modified, the 'R' was replaced to 'B' to show 'B****' and that was the special watch that he had for those kinds of people.

Posters.

I made contact with a man in Manchester who was selling posters. I went to England with the intention of buying a couple of hundred of them. When I got there, I saw the huge selection that he had but the minimum I could buy was 500 of each, anyway, I ended up buying 5000. The posters were probably the size of 30"x15" and one 500 pack was fairly heavy, not to mind 10 packs.

The fact that I was traveling with a suitcase was not going to stop me, I was convinced that this was money for old rope. Now the deal was done and I had my 5000 posters. The question was, how was I to take them to Ireland? There was not much help from the seller as he only took them to Liverpool and left them on the footpath for me. My plan was to try and get some truck driver to throw them in the truck and take them back by ferry to Dublin. It proved impossible to get any driver to do this since I had no invoice or no receipts and when there was no paper work for the customs, no one would take the chance since customs inspected all the vehicles entering the country.

There I was with my 5000 posters, sitting on the footpath thinking that the only person who could help me was God himself. Eventually, a man who was towing a caravan on his way to Ireland said he would put them in the caravan. I was most grateful, I could tell you. The man probably did not know how big of a chance he took because if caught, his car and caravan could have been seized by customs for carrying what would be termed commercial items.

As regards the 5000 posters, most of them outlived the artists. Some of the posters I can remember were of Shakin' Stevens, Adam Ant, Status Quo, and Metal Head or maybe it was Motor Head, well, it was some head anyway.

Fortune Telling Machines.

Fortune telling has always been exciting for the fans out there. Most people just cannot resist the wait to hear good news. There used to be a fortune telling machine which was owned by an old man. It worked on 10p, so there would not be much of a fortune to be made on it, even if it was going all the time. It had about six messages on the tape and when you put in your 10p coin, you'd get one of those messages. The machine would tell you something from you star sign, it really did not matter what sign you were, the 10p coin got it going and you sat there for 2 minutes listening to the good news and it then stopped.

The old man who owned the machine was always sitting beside it pretending to be asleep and sometimes he was but for most parts, he was awake, counting the 10p coins as they dropped in. He always knew the sound of the 10p coin because from time to time, people would try to put in a button or something similar in order to try to make it play. He would always wake up, open the machine and return to the culprit, whatever it was that they put in. He very seldom talked because it was his voice that was on the tape and it was an easily recognized voice.

One day, this lady who was big into fortune telling went through all the 6 messages and when she was not too happy with what she has heard, she gives the machine a kick. Now the sleeping man woke up very quickly, the woman burst out crying saying that the machine was not telling her anything of the truth. When the old man tried to console her, he only made things worse because she recognized his voice and she went into a right frenzy altogether then.

I learned something from that old man and it was the truest words that were ever spoken. He told me that you should never bring moneybags with you to a field day or a similar event because you might not get anything to put into the bags, how right he was, so many times.

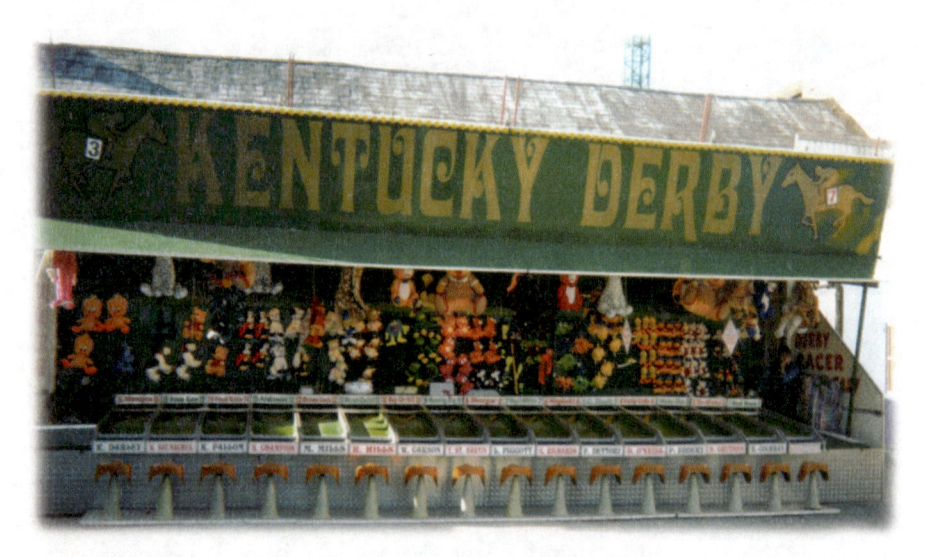

Above: Another Game of Skill. The Tommy & Linda Keyes Kentucky Derby

Left. A picture of the Cart Of Destinction as seen on the Late late Show

Tour De France, Cycle Race

Jesus, I must be drunk,
I see himself Working !!!

Michelle Campbell (Tyrone) & Caroline Murphy (Tipperary) pictured with the Sam Maguire - March 2004

Paddy Barry's Elaine Coughlan from Tipperary & the Holy Ground's Siobhan Quinn from Antrim

Left: The Speed Alert System As Seen On The Late Late Show

Candle Wax.

This idea looked good, you make a cast of a person's hand or foot in wax. It seemed easy to do, you just needed to apply oil to the foot or hand, dip it in the wax a few times and then remove it. You'd then have a cast of the foot or hand right down to the very last detail including fingerprints. I was thinking, if that person ever went missing, you had their identification already when starting the search.

Anyway, this looked like money for old rope, so all that was left to do was, as the Nike advert says, "Just Do It". A half-ton of wax was bought and shipped back to Ireland. It arrived in large slabs. Some new stainless steel melting pots were also bought for the project but unfortunately temperatures were not taken into consideration in the melting down of the wax. When melting of the wax was taking place, you often get a cloud of smoke similar to that used when electing a Pope, blue and white.

Trying to perfect the casts proved very difficult. With the wrong temperature of the melting wax and of course, the chance of getting burned after dipping your hand into the wax meant that you soon ran out of test victims. After further research, it was discovered that, you had to melt the wax slowly and it had to be kept at a temperature of less than 100 degrees. That meant that more stainless steel containers were needed and these had to have temperature gauges.

By this time, it looked like being another tried, tested but too slow to return money project. So it was shelved, I suppose you could say a cooling off period was needed! After a year or so has passed, I spotted a new idea which was in the form of scented candles. Since I had a half ton of the stuff, I thought I might get into the candle manufacturing business. All that I needed was wicks and scent, however, it was not as simple as you might think because wicks were hard to find and scents were very expensive.

An alternative had to be found and found it was. The wicks were substituted with twine and afterwards I realized, it was a great substitute. No place was ever burned down with those candles. It was Ireland's first safety Candle, it would light for about 3 seconds and then it went out, permanently.

As for the scent, well, the scent was added when they were put on display. Usually a quick spray of air freshener every hour or two, helped with the scent. Since then, I have noticed that scented candles have gotten more popular and I am sure that there are a lot more scents available now.

PS. How about inventing a safety candle, a flame without heat because naked flames are very dangerous and have caused many deaths or serious injuries.

Life Size Photos Of Famous People.

This was a simple operation, you stand beside a life size picture of a famous person, get your photo taken and hoped that whoever you are showing the photograph to is a bit blind. I tracked down the corporation behind the venture and was told they held the worldwide copyright on all pictures. However, they would be prepared to sell me a selection of ten life size photos for £4000.

They were located in London and I arranged to go and see them. When I got to London I was to telephone them to arrange to have me picked up. I get there and made my call. Shortly after and to my surprise, I was picked up in a Rolls Royce. I accepted the ride, sure, why wouldn't I. Now this Rolls was not in the best of shape, it was a gold rolls when it was first built but the years had taken it's toll on it and now it's color had faded to yellow, just like the yellow cab.

It was raining and the wipers did not work but we got to the headquarters of the worldwide distribution center of the life size pictures. It was located down a back lane, where there were a lot of cars being repaired. At least, they were in the right locality to keep the roller ticking over. The office was upstairs I can remember that any views from where I was sitting, was of cars being repaired and sprayed.

As soon as I arrived, I was met by the 'Del Boy' sales team, the phone was ringing and orders were coming in from all over the world, Australia, Hong Kong, and the USA. They all called within a few minutes and they were not just looking for ten items, no, they were looking for 50 to 100 at each location. Of course, while I was there, a call came in from Ireland.

That budding entrepreneur then informed the telephone caller that they were just too late and that the new franchise owner was sitting in front of them at corporate headquarters and had signed exclusive rights to operate for Ireland. This was news to me because I had signed nothing. Anyway the next move required by me was a cash deposit, as since I was not carrying enough cash, arrangements were made to take me to the bank in the roller for a withdrawal.

As I was hesitating a bit, the offers were getting better. Instead of 10 life-size photos, I was now going to be given two extra, one of Margaret Thatcher and one of the Queen. In my mind, I was thinking that those two would be a great help to my business, especially around the 12th. of July.

I was wondering what was going to happen next, I told them that I was going to be staying over night and if I decided to buy, I would go to the bank myself, in the morning. The Del Boy team told me that tomorrow was going to be too late, it's now or never. As a result, the rolls was not available to take me away, instead a transit van that was leaving one of the repair shops, took me back to the tube station.

Anyway, I returned to Dublin and after looking up a few magazines, I got a few pictures of Barry McGuigan, Samantha Fox, the Pope, Mohammad Ali and a few more and I got them blown up to life size. These cost me around £200, which beats £4000 anytime. This selection worked for a Summer or two and that was the end of that venture.

Sand Art.

This simple operation looked easy to manage, colored sand, just put it into bottles or plastic containers and there it was. However, the plan was to do this in Ireland and the sand was in the USA and it's hard to take enough sand in a suitcase for the summer season. An easy way for me would just buy some coloring and color the sand myself. Like everything, this was not going to be that simple, the first place I looked for coloring was in the construction industry.

There was some coloring available however, they were only in black or brown which is not very colorful. After further searching, yellow was found and that particular yellow was the coloring used for painting lines on the roads. This was a major breakthrough but I still hadn't enough colors. Eventually, more colors were found. I thought I was nearly there but coloring sand, especially during the wet Summers wasn't the easiest thing to do. I'd leave the sand outside the house to dry only to have a shower come along and destroy everything again. The system was not working because it was not drying quickly enough.

A new drying system was needed and very soon a drying plan was put into operation. Sand and coloring was mixed put into bags and put in a spin dryer to dry. It worked reasonably well until the bag burst, now, spin dryer not working either.

Finally the code was cracked. I found a hotel that were using a drying system for drying sheets, etc., so I was able to leave a few boxes of sand there to dry and everything worked out fine in the end.

Paint Like Picasso.

'Fun for kids, paint like Picasso'. This was a simple operation, a plain piece of white paper was placed on a frame that spun around. It sometimes spun too fast to paint like Picasso but anyway, you poured the paint onto the spinning paper, splashing the paint all over it. Indeed, the child as well, was sometimes part of your finished product. The result should have been a 6"x6" piece of wet paper covered in different colors and this would have been similar to Picasso's work, no doubt.

This operation created a lot of work not just for the operator but for the mothers of the kids in trying to remove paint from their hands and clothes. If one had the insight to include face painting with the Picasso painting, extra income could have been generated and that would have taken care of some of the complaints. The mothers often cried 'look at him, he has paint all over him, even his face'. I'd reply, just for scutting, 'Doesn't he look lovely!'

Traveling To Festivals.

Working at fairs and festivals can be fun if you are going there and not bothered too much about making money. I remembered what the old man said to me 'You would be well advised not to bring any moneybags because you most likely will have nothing to put into the bags, by the time you get finished'.

If you were lucky enough to have something that did work for you and you took some money with you, you very soon had some new friends. I remember being at a festival and hearing the sad story of a van breaking down a few miles outside town. The van was full of 8 track stereos and they were the DVD's of that time.

I was promised to be given a couple of stereo's once I got the van into town but £40 was needed to buy a battery to get her running. After further pleading and promises from the vendor, I gave him £20 towards the new battery, needless to say he did not seem to find me as easily when he got the van going and there was no sign of the stereo's either.

Well a year later at the same town at the same festival we met again, I said to him, 'how are the stereo's going?' 'Great' says he, 'how many do you want?' 'How is the battery in your van?' I asked. 'Very good' says he. 'Do you remember me at all from last year?' I inquired. 'How could I forget' he says. 'Well, I gave you £20 towards the battery and you never gave the money back to me.' 'Oh' he says, 'was it you that gave me that money, I could never remember who it was'.

'Well do you know, there was no luck attacked to it at all, on my way to buy the battery, I went to the off-license and bought some cheap wine. I got a bit drunk, ended up breaking a window, resisting arrest and I got 6 months in jail, all over that £20 you gave me'.

I just walked away and I was thinking what excellent value everyone got for that £20 that I gave him. He was off the streets for 6 months and that must have been worth a lot to many people.

Snooker Tables.

The snooker table business was big business. There was a shortage of tables earlier on when it became popular on TV. Steve Davis then was the hero, every child wanted to be him or Hurricane Higgins. I started out by going to England and buying small 6'x3' and 7'x4' tables. These would be most suitable for home use. They were put into bedrooms, garages, sitting rooms, kitchens and attics, oddly enough, most houses did not have room for them but that was not going to stop them from getting one.

There were usually disagreements and brawls with the women of the house and their argument was that this snooker table was taking up valuable space in the sitting room, or some other place she claimed was her territory, before this table arrived. With the women getting their way, the tables usually ended up, outside in a shed or garage. The demand for snooker tables coming up to Christmas was huge, everyone seemed to want them. I remember a day or two before Christmas, I would have sold 50 more tables if I had them. With Santa Claus and the last minute shoppers' panic the cry was 'what are we going to do?'.

'We promised Johnny or Tommie a table', they'd say, 'I have to get it'. Well, I took the name and phone numbers of the 10 most desperate needing tables and assured them that I would have a table for them a couple of days after Christmas. That, I was hoping, was going to save everyone so I head for London two days after Christmas in my Hiace to buy 12 tables.

On my way to London, a snow storm came and a lot of snow fell. Now, trying to find your way in the snow is not that easy because I had to get out of a van every so often and clean off the signs, to see what direction I had to go. This was not easy but it had to be done. I managed to pick up the tables and start back for Holyhead. It was snowing all the ways and when I got there, I found out that the ferry had been cancelled. It had not left Dublin the evening before and it would have taken a while for the ferry to be back in Holyhead again. Of course, the right thing to do would have been to stay in Holyhead, but no, I headed off for Liverpool because I knew that that ship was sailing. With the snowing conditions getting worse, the police decided to close down the motorway and I being half ways down to Liverpool.

Anyway, they directed me off the motorway to a place called Ryhl in Wales. The place that I got to stay was at a seaside resort.

Now, judging by the amount of clothes that was on the bed, they were still operating in the Summer time zone. It was absolutely freezing and after spending two nights at the artic, the roads were opened again and I headed off for Liverpool and caught the ferry back to Dublin.

When I arrived back in Dublin, most places were closed due to the snow, for this was a major snowstorm. I started making my phone calls to arrange the deliveries. Not one of the ten, that had ordered them, wanted them because Santa Claus had brought something else. The snooker starvation before Christmas was over and the great demand had now past.

Just wait till Christmas comes around again as it does every year. I now had 12 tables but I did manage to sell them over the next couple of months. I had seen the great demand that was there for the tables and felt the pain I went through getting them so I was thinking, why don't I make them by myself. I took one of the tables apart to see what was in them, so my plan was to source these various parts and go into production myself.

Now remember that there was no Internet available at that time and everything had to be done via the phone. You'd call a manufacturer or write to them and wait for a reply and that usually hardly ever came. The green baise I found after a long search but that was the easy part. I now had to find the rubber for the cushions. This proved to be a real problem, I tried old cycle tubes that I folded over but this did not work. I started to make more phone calls to different rubber manufacturers in different parts of the country and indeed, outside the country as well. Some places were looking for £3,000 or more upfront to make a mould that they could then use to manufacture it. I simply did not have that kind of money, so the search continued until I got a tip that, there was a place in the South of Ireland making rubber, so I went there.

There was rubber there alright, enough to make tires for every car in the country. That was no good, so I had to go to another place in the Midlands. I looked for the production manager and I was assured that he would help me out. The only problem was that he was in Wales and would be back in Ireland again in a month. I got in the van and started out straight for Wales. When I got to the rubber centre, there were rolls and rolls of rubber and all of it not suitable, no progress was made there either.

I returned home and started buying old broken down pool tables to get the rubber that was uses in them. I tried to stretch it, so as to get the most out of the rubber but the problem was that when the rubber was stretched, when the ball hit off the cushion, it could go in any direction, it's crazy snooker.

With a ball acting like ping-pong, it's no good for the serious players. I remember then going into a place in Dublin, that was selling medical products, with a piece of L shaped rubber. Standing at the counter one of the Dubs said 'can I help you?' I said, 'I was told you sell rubber here', he said, 'no, we don't but I can tell you where to get it'. Needless to say, my eyes lit up and I was thinking progress at last. Could I believe what I was hearing?. There was a place on this earth it did not matter to me, where it was, I was going to get it.

He replied 'it grows on tress in Singapore, it's all over the place'. I left, no, not for Singapore. I thought it was a joke but believe it or not, the Dublin man was right. I eventually found someone in Britain that was importing L shaped rubber from Singapore and I was able to buy it at a reasonable enough price.

Now after that long search for the rubber, nothing could be as hard to find again. The corners did prove difficult but I found someone that made them for me, they were just L shaped brackets. Next up were the pockets, (the nets) these were difficult to find so I had to come up with an alternative. I got some string vests, cut them up and sewed them together. There you had your pockets and they worked fine.

At this stage, I now had most of the parts needed to make the tables so the 'Just do it' manufacturer was about to begin. I made the first table and it was a little difficult to play on but as time went by, the tables and the playing got better.

After a while, slate tables were being made. Now, those were heavy and they could not be moved around easily, basically, wherever you set them up you left them there. I then started making snooker tables in a way that, you could turn them into dining room tables. After you finished dinner, you just turned it over and played snooker and when finished with that, just spin it back again. It was a simple thing but it took a lot of effort to get it to work smoothly.

After that, it was time to turn my attention to the full size table of 12'x6'. Remember, this was a thing that nobody would attempt because it was only a master craftsman that could make a snooker and billiard table. However, I was going to change that myth. The slate used was in Italy but I had found a place in England that was importing it, so I was able to get it from there.

Again with the Hiace, I'd go and get the slate for the table and take it back. The slate weighed a ton and a quarter. With the 5 slabs of slate, it was difficult to move and I needed strong men to help me take it out of the van. Fortunately, I had some good friends that were always available to help me out.

This master craft took me a little while to perfect and as regards some of the tables I made, well, let's just say, the home team might have had the advantage. The players would soon know the 'easy pockets' and gravity as opposed to skill would help them win games. The level on a full size snooker table always needed some time to settle down, however, some tables to this day, are still settling.

You were strongly advised not to hit the ball too hard as it could easily jump off the table and hit a window or a wall and this would not be necessarily a trick shot. The small snooker table market was still going strong but the only problem was, the old story that they were in the way in most houses. Putting them in a bedroom was the last resort so an idea came to me, how about a snooker table you could change into a bed!

A great idea was born, this combo table was going to be the makings of many new World Champions in the future. The bed part was to be used as the base and when you were finished playing snooker, you'd simply tuck the snooker table top under the bed. My grand idea was to have a snooker table in every bedroom in Ireland. It did not happen, I only made a few and they are now collector's items.

World Snooker Champion.

During the making of the snooker tables, there was always a couple of tables available for a game. The staff from other nearby businesses would often be over to play a game of snooker. One of the business owners decided that we should have an world snooker competition. He would be the self-appointed representative for Dublin and the tournament would have been against the Culchies. There was to be a £1 fee per game and we were to have at least a game or two played everyday. The first player to reach 20 wins, would get the money.

The money was folded and stuck into a beam in the ceiling. Every day, the world waited to see who would first take the title of 'the champion of Kimmage' and then world champion after that. Eventually, the day of reckoning came and in the final the expected winner had his supporters all gathered around. Well, he did win and he paraded around the table with the cue high over his head chanting that, he was 'the Dub that beat the Culchie world champion'. Now, the best part of all this was the culchie money winnings. He starts to remove the notes from the beam. He could see the edges of his twenty pound notes and his eyes were lit up like a Christmas tree.

The glee soon turned to anger because the culchies had pulled a fast one. Someone has sliced one of the pound notes into strips and had pocketed the rest of the money. The 'world champion' had been conned, 'those bleedin' culchies again' he roared. This was priceless, the embarrassment had set in because he had already made plans on how to spend his winnings. He told us how the £20 was going to be put on a horse, a dead cert.

This act was never forgiven and is still talked about to this day.

Weight In The Cue.

In the snooker business, when selling the tables you would always be asked about cues. What was the best cue to use so on and so forth. Some of the cues you'd buy were not much better than a handle for a brush with a point on one end. However, with the standard of playing not always being that of world class, you would get by with it.

Some people took great care of their cue's, making or buying cases to hold them, soft cases for the gentle players and hard cases for the good players. I knew of one man and I'm sure, there were many more that used to sleep with his cue. I guess he loved his cue. Now, the good players, well, the ones that thought they were good, they all had their own special cue and they all had their own case. They were always minded it as if they were a gold rods and some even kept them at a certain temperature, all year round.

I remember one time been given a cue to take to Dublin to get an extra 2oz in weight put into the handle. Now this would have been a specialized job and great care had to be taken regarding the weight of the cue. The owner of this cue had tipped himself as one day becoming the world champion and he just needed the extra 2oz to get more power in his shots just for that extra control of the ball. I had the intended to drop off the cue to the specialist when I got to Dublin on Monday morning and have it back down the country again to its owner by the weekend, for an important tournament.

Well, I forgot all about it until I found it on the floor of the van on the Saturday morning, when at that time, I should have been picking it up to take it back down the country. This was an emergency, drastic action was called for. Well, I was thinking that, sure it was only a matter of adding 2oz extra so why not do it myself. I had solved bigger problems that that before. I got a 3/8" drill bit and drilled a hole about 3" deep into the end of the cue. I then got a 6" nail and cut 3" off it and dropped it into the handle. I finished it off by putting some wood filler in and then took it back to him. 'A great job', the man said. He won many tournaments afterwards with that cue but he did not become the world champion as he had expected.

One night, while watching the closing stages of the world championship, I overheard one woman saying to the other, is that snooker just played by dummies, since no one talks to the other at all.

Speed Systems.

This was first displayed on the Late Late Enterprise Show and there were probably about a hundred other different new inventions on show that night. There were a lot of smart business people there and many of them with long and successful careers. The speed system was a safety system that indicate to motorists what speed they were doing and encouraged them to slow down in certain areas. A panel of judges at the show liked the system so much that they gave it the first prize and this prize consisted of a complete package of office supplies, Laptop computer, phones, fax machines and much more.

My next job now was, to learn how to use this equipment and today, my speed systems are installed in many parts Ireland. The next new safety system of mine was aimed at the pedestrians. Now, pedestrian crossings can sometimes be dangerous places and most pedestrians must think so too because they usually cross some distance away from the crossing. A new safer pedestrian crossing was developed and it consisted of count down clocks to show the pedestrian how much time they had to cross the road. There were flashing amber lights embedded into the roadway, to warn oncoming drivers that someone about to cross.

A additional warning and safety voice message could also be included. These safety features could still be included in existing pedestrian crossings so the market for this system is huge.

Umpire Assist.

This system can be used to help clarify in a game of football or hurling whether a point was scored or not. The netting used is practically invisible and it stands about 3 feet back from the goalpost uprights. After the match, it can be removed since there is a sliding rail attached to each post for easy removal and installation. This is not intended to make umpires redundant but would be a great help also for under age games. Another benefit would be that it would speed up the game since the ball would be right beside the goalkeeper after most scores. For further details and information about this system, you can go to www.sportspeedsystems.com.

I am often asked about different things that people would have in there minds and they ask me, 'where do I go to start?' The starting off is not the most difficult part, it what comes after that can be the problem, to sell your product and that means marketing and by that, I don't mean taking it into town on a market day.

You just need to go out there and "Just Go And Do It". Afterwards you might say that it maybe was a mistake but never the less, you did it. To me, there's no such thing as failure. The person that never made a mistake in his life, probably never made anything. It's also true to say that the person that made too many mistakes probably never made anything either.

The Taxi.

There are many people I need to thank from working on the taxi side of things, first up is Wayne McCulla of Yellow Cab. Many years ago, I walked into the Yellow Cab office and he gave me a job with no experience whatsoever. I didn't knowing a single street or building in Boston and what a pain that was for everyone but since then, curiosity and understanding had led me to know the town now.

I would like to thank Mary Allstop and the dispatchers and the staff at Yellow Cab for all they have done for me.

I would also like to thank the Bar Owners and Staff of the following pubs in Quincy.

Sarsfields
Declan Kelly, Michelle Campbell, Mary Kavanagh, Angie, Mary Ellen, Deirdre, Angie and Kevin.

Paddy Barry's and the Holy Ground
Gerry Hanley, Siobhan, Liam, Toby, Adrian, Joanne, Emer, Catherine and Elaine.

Bad Abbott's
Peter and Ann Kerr, Sonny and all the staff and the Celtic supporters lead by Shane and Bernie.

The Half Door
Kevin McGrath and all the staff

The Goalpost
Joe Mulkerns Staff and customers

Also these other bars,
Malacky's, Delaney's, The Irish Pub, Murphy's Twin Shamrock, Darby's, The Pres Pub, Cronin's, all of which have been wonderful to me down through the years. I hope that I was of some help to them and their wonderful customers and long may it continue into the future.

Arriving In The USA.

Arriving in the USA in the early Seventies was a major move for me because when you went to the USA, you were most likely going to be there for a long time and probably make it your new home for the rest of your life. To put enough money together or borrow it for the trip took an awful long time. After I got to the States, the only communication with home was by letter and I'd be looking forward to the news from the football or hurling matches, once a month.

There was no Setanta Sports Channel in these times or the Internet either, I remember one time hearing the result of a football final in the Seventies on American radio and it said 'Mr. Offaly beat Mr. Kerry on points', this was included in some sports news and it was a big break in announcing Irish sports results in the USA. I hope that the announcer realizes now that he was talking about counties as opposed to men. To hear the mention of anything else other than basketball or ice hockey was an absolute pleasure.

After being in the USA for some time and finding out about the way things work, I eventually got around to making a phone call home but this was very difficult. This came under the heading International Calls and you needed lots of time to make that call. You had to collect loads of quarters, made contact with the telephone exchange operator and they in turn got in contact with the international operator, you then gave them the number.

At that time, when you put the money in, the phones would only take about 8 quarters at a time so you had to put the money in, maybe 4 times and it cost $8 or $9 for a 3 minute call. You then had to wait for the call to be connected and that was not a nice wait because, if you did not get through, it was good bye to your money and the phone call. There were no mobiles nor phone cards at that time and thank heavens that things have changed so much for the better.

Afraid To Eat.

I remember that after arriving in the USA, I was afraid to order food in a restaurant because I was only used to bread and butter and of course, bacon and cabbage. It was plain food that I was used to and that's what I wanted, unfortunately, most of what was on offer was not that plain and I was a bit skeptical about it and to this day, I still am.

When working some days, someone would be going to the fast food joint for a meal and they would offer to get me something. Now, up to that time, I don't think I had ever eaten even a burger but hunger sometimes makes you change your ways. I relented and ordered a burger, of course, I did not like it. With the green leaves and red sauce on it, it was far too exotic for me and of course, not having been brave enough to ask for it plain, very few burgers were eaten for a long time.

Every time I used to be asked, did I want French fries, 'French Fries, Oh no', I would say. This went on for a long time until one day, while sitting outside eating at lunch time, someone said 'here, have some French fries, try them, you might like them'. Now, I know they looked like, what we called chips, only smaller, 'match sticks' I called them for a long time.

I had just found out what French fries were and I was kicking myself because I had refused them for so long. I thought what people were saying was 'French Flies' and I had heard about the French eating snails and frogs and I was not going to take a chance on these French Flies.

Immigration.

To go to the USA in the Sixties or Seventies, you had to go to the USA Embassy and get a visa. You applied for the visa and then you were called for an interview. You were questioned regarding your trip and if everything went well, you got your visa which was good for 6 months. When those 6 months was coming to an end, you could apply for an extension for another six months which, you usually got. This was good because it gave you a chance to get someone to sponsor you for permanent residency.

I remember one time, arriving at immigration and at the time, the amount of money you had with you coming into the country would be stamped on your passport. Now, I had after a long struggle but managed to put together £100 so I came up with the idea that it would be better for me to go to two banks with the vast sum of money that I had. Maybe, I was not sure of the currency exchange or what I could take out of the country, so I went to one bank with my £50 and I got $75 in return, that amount of money was then stamped on my passport. Then, I headed off to another bank with the other £50 and I got another $75. The difference here was that they never bothered to stamp the amount on money on my passport.

When I arrived in the States, I was going through immigration when the immigration officer looks at my passport and sees the $75 stamped on it. He asked me how much money I had, I told him that I had $150. He pointed out to me saying that my passport only stated $75, I told him my story of the two banks, how one stamped the amount and the other did not. His next question was directed on how long I intended to stay in the USA. I told him '6 months'. '6 months', says he, '6 months and $150?'. 'Yes,' says I. 'Well, I want you to come back in 6 months time and tell me, how you managed to live here for 6 months, on $150'.

Well, when the six months were up, I returning but there was no sign of him. If he was there, I could have shown him the miracle of how the $150 had changed into about $2000. Many years later, the 90 day visitor visa was introduced that was a great help because it meant, not having to go to the embassy and life was made easier for everyone.

The green slip that was given to you when going to the States was your tracking number and if that was returned to the Aer Lingus desk, it meant you had left the States. Many people come and went, at their leisure for a good part of their lives. I was told once and it was good advise, only answer the question you are asked and don't go on adding to the answer. I always found that, if you answered the first two or three questions, you were, as they might say, in the USA, 'all set'.

Now, if you are found to be carrying around 6 months of pills while going on a week or ten days holidays, you might have some explaining to do. I knew of people that came to the USA on holidays, only to take, what you would describe as items that you would not need for a week's holiday, items such as a 3 months supply of Lyon's or Barry's tea, phone books and coffee. You name it and they took it with them but for the most part, they got through.

Immigration were always on the look out for certain age groups, such as young men in their twenties. These lads would be described as 'Aer Lingus Painters' and the girls in their twenties, would be classified under what used to be called operation 'Nab A Nanny'.

That was then but now it is different. September 11th. 2001 changed everything and now it is much more difficult to travel. There are extra checks to be done and you are going to be tracked every time you travel. This travel will be logged and there's going to be no way of hiding where you've been and that means that you are going to be restricted in your movements unless of course, you have all the necessary documents in proper order. Unfortunately, not everyone would be in that position, so you are going to have to stay wherever you are, like it or not.

Things have definitely changed for everyone regarding travel. Young people are restricted in their travel but it was unheard of 20 years ago, for you to have a visit from your family back in Ireland. Now it's common practice for brothers, sisters, Mothers and Fathers all coming on a visit to the USA. In fact, it is not uncommon to be introduced, when they arrived in the States, to 'This is my Mother and this her Boyfriend', followed a few weeks later by, 'This is my Father and this is his Girlfriend'. How things have changed in the last 20 years.

The visit of a close relative is always nice, especially if you are not able to travel yourself, for some reason or other. Unfortunately, it can be very expensive if you need to take time off from work, indeed I know, two weeks of entertaining would take its toll on anyone's finances. As one person told me some time ago, 'if I knew it was going to cost so much, I would have just sent the money and they could have gone to Australia for the month. Just send me a card to let me know how things are going'.

Fortunately, that would not be the general view on all those relatives that would be visiting.

Visiting The Uncle In The USA.

I have seen some difficulty with people coming to visit their uncles and aunts. The invitation to come over to the States would have been made sometime in the past when they themselves visited Ireland. However, they were only kids back then and sure the invitation would never have been accepted anyway. It has often times happened that, fifteen years later, that same invitation would now be accepted.

The little kids grow up pretty fast now-a-days and its not like the old times when coming over meant on the slow boat, seven days traveling to USA. It's now not more that 6 hours travel and they are there. They arrive to be greeted with 'O My God, you grew so big, what do they feed you on? Flowering Spuds.' Some others would hear 'aren't you just great to come over and who are these other people with you?' 'Oh, this is my girlfriend and the other two are our new neighbors, they're from Africa originally, they won't stay too long, they are used to staying in a hotel!' I bet, the next time they go to Ireland, they'll keep their mouth shut.

This particular conversation continued, 'They're only out for a week, to check on what's available here, for the poor and the underprivileged. Anything at all, is good enough for us, don't worry about us, we will be fine.' The reply was 'No problem, you are all very welcome, tell us all the news from the old country, tell us, who lives in Mike's old place now?' 'Oh, there's new people living there now, from somewhere in Africa.' 'Did your father say anything about the few acres that was left to me many years ago?, I might go back and build there soon. I heard that property is worth a lot in the Old Country' 'Yes', he said, 'have a look at the video he sent over for you to have a look at, it's called, the field.'

You might want to give your return more thought because there are some Bull McCabes around. They have a slight veneer of a covering but underneath they are the same.

Now, after the welcome was over, the visitors from Ireland might have trouble trying to understand why everyone was in bed by 9 or 10 o'clock every night and getting up at 5am. These people were more inclined to be heading out for the night at 10pm and coming back close to the time that the uncle would be thinking of getting up out of bed.

Young people coming here often get the impression that the USA is under some kind of Marshall law regarding the buying of alcohol. They could find themselves staying in what is called a "Dry Town", which would be a Town that does not sell alcohol. Also, when they go to a bar, their ID is checked at the door and again at the bar. There would often be complaints when they would not be allowed to take the open bottles of alcohol outside. The bar would be closed down for maybe a week for letting that happen. "Get us back to the Quays and Supermacs" you'd hear them say.

The next problem could be arriving in at 3 or 4 am singing 'the streets of New York' after a night of drinking inspired by the sight of The Big Yellow Taxis outside in the street, I'm sure 'Uncle Benjy' upstairs might not take kindly when awakened a few of hours before his rising time. This can cause a lot of disagreement and arguments.

As a result, I have even taken people in my taxi at 3 and 4am in the morning, to Motels and sometimes to the airport, with the only words spoken 'we will never go back there again' or 'wait until they come back to Ireland' which will probably be never. I am sure that everything works out in the end, time heals most wounds.

Football And Hurling.

Football and Hurling is a great social outlet, a good footballer or hurler over in the States would be well looked after. Well, better than back home in Ireland. Help would be given in getting a job, finding a place to stay and giving some money to get them by for a while. The playing field could be a place that some old scores could be settled and you could have neighbors from back home playing for different teams. It's been known that even brothers could be playing for different teams and anything from the past that should have been sorted out then between the neighboring factions, this was the opportunity to get even on the neutral ground.

I was at a match many years ago and the hard man of that time had taken up a position beside the umpire. He warned the umpire that lifting the white flag too often was a dangerous thing to do, when he was around. Things were not going well for the angry man's team and he said to the umpire 'if you lift that flag once again, I will kill you, because the last four points you gave, were wides.' On the next attack, a goal was scored, another man shouted over to the angry man, 'the players must have heard you, they're putting the ball in the net for you, to see for yourself'.

Attacked.

A few years back, I remember a young Irish man coming out of a bar when he was attacked and robbed by a colored man. Two other fellows saw it happen and ran out of the bar with their hurling sticks. They then started to beat the colored man around the street with the hurleys. When the police were called, the battered man just sat there and he was asked for descriptions of his attackers. He said 'two white men dressed in blue and yellow and carrying large wooden spoons attacked me, they came out of a bar and restaurant'. The police said that, they might have been chefs, when they had spoons with them.

I believe the search continues to this day for those fugitives. I did not hear of any ransom being offered for their capture. I would expect that they have fled the jurisdiction by now, it was rumored that the FBI have searched the Glen of Atherlow and the Burren, without any success so it's now in the Cold Case Files.

New Arrivals.

If young Irish people are going to continue to come to the USA, something needs to be done on the immigration side. It is not what the young people want, 90 days and then return, there are many places for them to go. It's different now compared with the 50's and 60's when there was only one or two places that you could go. Now, with travel the way it is, there's all of Europe that can be explored, not to mention Australia where the young people are going by the thousands.

Indeed those people are well educated and are valued workers. There are many young Irish people, having years of education, now doing jobs that does not require the qualifications they have. It's time that Irish groups get together and put pressure on the politicians to do what is needed. We need to make those already there and recognize the talents of those coming to the USA.

Some may say that those coming over now are much different than those who came 20 years ago. Well, of course, they are different, painting and babysitting is not their only talent, some will say that they are better at drinking or socializing and don't care too much about the work. I am sure it can be very frustrating if you are restricted in what you can do.

Twenty-five years ago, I knew people that were just as good at drinking and socializing as the young people of today. They are now owners of large construction companies or bars and have become millionaires. They were all young and foolish at one time.

American Women.

The young Irish man, arriving in the USA was often a sought after species for the young American lady. Some of the young Irish men regarded it as a way to obtain a green card. The wedding bells would soon ring. The magic of that brogue. 'I love that brogue. I heard that so many times' and I always say, you could get tired of it very soon. The answer is always the same, 'I would never get tired listening to that'.

Unfortunately, it does not seem that way and they grow tired very quickly of that brogue. Returning home from work after a pit stop at the bar, with the dinner on the table, after a few times and the dinner not being eaten, things can change very quickly.

Look up the Internet for information on changing a man and you'll probably find no help there. You could call his mother for some guidance but you'll not get much help from that side either. 'His father done it all his life, came home when Man United lost, so get used to it'. Problem here in the States is 'we need to talk'. 'Ok, talk'. The promises made will then last up until the sobering process kicks in and then normal service is resumed again.

I have heard it said, 'she loves Ireland' so many times, 'we are going back to live in Ireland'. I always ask 'when were you there?' and the answer is usually 'July or August, it was awesome'. She says that, she cannot get back, quick enough and I am there thinking to myself, 'try January, February or March and see how awesome it is then'.

I have heard of young Irish men returning to Ireland with their new American wife. sometimes to a country area or even on an island, back to the place where their ancestors came from. You'd hear them recalling the story of their Grandmother and Grandfather who came to the New World on the Titanic but had to swim some of the way since the ship did not make it all the way to the dock in New York.

It's a great story, so let's go back. No doubt some American wives may well be settling in but after a few weeks of their nails getting long or maybe the sun tan wearing off , together with living on an island, the cry would be heard, 'where do I get my nails done?' The tough Islander would reply, 'You will need to get the boat to go to the mainland but in this bad weather, you might have to let them grow a little bit longer. I guarantee you that, relocation plans would be started well before the weather improves.

Going back to her roots, the land of the ancestor's, no longer looks as good and a return to the best country in the world awaits her. At least she now thinks she knows why her ancestors left Ireland in the first place. America, the land of Freedom, the place where you can get the important things in life done, your nails and, of course, the sun bed for your body in January and February.

The Big Dig.

The Big Dig was a massive undertaking through the city of Boston. A mile and a half of underground tunnel that sometimes came up to ground level and then went back down, it was a huge job altogether. Thousands of workers were supposed to be working at it but it was hard to see them as they were hidden away working underground. The job was initially supposed to cost 3 billion dollars but at the last count, it had topped the 14 billion dollar mark. You know, it would have been cheaper to build a new city outside Boston, then, we would have no need for the Big Dig.

The traffic disruption it caused was a constant nightmare. Day or night, it did not matter, one day you would be going one way and the next day, the barrels would be moved and you were directed in the other direction. Often, you'd be stuck for hours on end in traffic.

The police, well, they'd just directed you away from where they were and for the most part you'd finish up somewhere lost. 'Don't bother us asking directions, most of it is complete now, maybe only another year or two. What's another year'. Even this new wonder of the World, traffic is easily disrupted. I traveled three thousand miles recently in six hours to Boston, however, the fifteen miles I traveled from Logan to home took another three hours.

Even after ten years, it still is not completed. With the 14 billion dollars they spent, you would think that they would spend some of the money on painting lines on the road, just to help keep the drivers in their lanes during traffic.

When you come out on the north side of the tunnel you'll see a beautiful bridge and definitely, in that part of the road, a few white lines would help. Is there not an Albert Reynolds over here? Albert, when Minister once said, that he would go and paint the lines himself, if they needed to be done.

Well after all the hype and there was lots of it and after spending the 14 billion the tunnel is almost complete, well, at least you can drive through it now. They are still not finished but the traffic is flowing better now.

I was recently taking four people from Quincy to Brighton, which meant going through the mega tunnel. The two men were from Cork and the two women were American. When entering this fine tunnel, the lights alone were a sight to see, the two American women were really impressed saying something like 'isn't this awesome, Awesome, O My God'.

'Hi boys, did you ever see anything like this before?', said the women. The two boys were not as impressed as the women and were asking what all the commotion was about. They told the ladies, 'You never saw our tunnel, the Jack Lynch tunnel'. They tried to explain that Jack Lynch was not a baseball player but used a piece of wood called a Hurley. Now explaining to the girls, what hurling was, took some time. At the end, they told the two women that the Big Dig was only a small job, in comparison to the Jack Lynch tunnel.

They explained that the tunnel back home had a Dunkin' Donut, McDonalds and a Bank, it also goes all the way from Cork to Kerry, a distance of about sixty miles and it goes right through the lakes of Killarney. On top of that, it took only about six months to complete. They further added that a new construction has now started, a tunnel from Ireland to the USA, now how awesome is that?, big dig, how are ya!.

P.S. As part of the Big Dig, one of the tunnels across to Logan Airport is called The Ted Williams Tunnel after the great baseball player. Jack Lynch in Ireland was a great hurler and the Jack Lynch tunnel is called after him.

Driving Licenses.

Now-a-days, driving is a must, you just cannot get around with any comfort unless you drive. Now most people that arrive here from Ireland would have not much more than a provisional license. Certainly, it's a start, but it's not what is required by the law over in the States. The fear of being stopped is always present and if you are driving, you'd better watch yourself and make sure that you do not break any rules of the road. Stop, in this country means stop, none of this changing down to third gear and tearing through doing forty. There'll be no running of the red lights and forget about driving if you have drink taken, take yellow cab, that's what it's there for.

However, if you are ever stopped, and you don't have the proper documentation, you better hope that the officer's grandparents came from the old country. Now, if you are stopped by a state trooper, be prepared for a big ticket, they don't write small ones because their time is to precious. You are also highly advised not to say anything and if you are asked a question your answer better be 'Yes' because anything else, you'll finish up with a bigger ticket so silence is the best policy.

I know of a young Irish man that was here for a few weeks and when he had a bit of courage in him, he decided that he would take the girlfriend's car to the local store. He made it to the store all right, done his shopping and returned to the car. Forgetting where he was and dreaming of the homeland, he started to drive on the left hand side of the street, now, this is something you can easily do, as I know myself, if you have driven on the left all your life. You would not ever do it, if there is traffic but when the road is quiet, you can easily go the wrong side of the street until you see another car coming towards you.

Well, back to our boy, he was motoring down the road, as happy as Larry, when who does he meet, the State Trooper and he coming straight for him. With lights flashing, siren blaring and probably contacting the Pentagon too, our Irish driver came to an immediate stop when he realized that he was in the wrong.

With the trooper standing outside the window, the Irish lad had a hard time trying to figure out how to let down the glass. He eventually managed to let it down and the trooper growls 'where were you going?' 'Back to my girlfriend's flat' was the reply. 'Back to girlfriend's flat, what's a flat?' the trooper enquired, 'Where she lives' said the young fellow, who at this stage was a whiter shade of pale. 'Is this your car?' 'No' 'Give me your license and registration?' 'I don't have a license and I don't know what the other thing your looking for is'.

'Get out of the car' the trooper roared. 'Sorry sir, I know now what I did was wrong but sir, where I came from, I was told to always remember that when driving, that left was right and right was wrong, so I just forgot where I was'.

The trooper's ancestors must have definitely been from the old country because he told him to leave that car where it was and start walking back to the girlfriend's apartment. He could then get her to come and pick it up and the officer warned the driver not to ever go out on the street again without the proper documentation.

Drunk, In The Snow.

One bitterly cold night, the temperature was a low 17° and there was about two feet of snow lying on the ground, I got a phone call from a bar saying that my assistance was required as someone over visiting had taken a little too much drink. With anybody visiting, I would not usually say that they were drunk, they're just a little tired after their long trip.

Well, in this case, the man in question was drunk. Now, this character was over visiting his brother and oddly enough, the brother seemed OK. After a lot of work getting out visitor into the taxi, accompanied by the brother, we went off on a journey that was not very long, about 10 minutes. However, in that 10 minutes, things happened. The visitor had passed out completely and the brother had joined him. They were united together now in blissful hibernation.

I arrived at the address they told me to go, that was when they were conscious. Now, my work started in earnest and that was in trying to wake them up. I started with the one that was awake at the start, shall we say, the resident brother. After a long time huffing and puffing, I eventually got him out of the car and dragged him through the snow, up three or four steps on to a porch and left him there. I then went back to get the visitor out of the car, I dragged him too out of the car, across the road and up to where the brother was. As this was going on, it was closing time and I had got three or four other calls from people that were not quite as inebriated but I needed to go and pick them up too and take them home.

I asked the resident brother, did he have his keys to get into the apartment, he indicated that he had and with that, I told them that I had to go and pick up a few customers that were waiting for me.

'Yes we're ok, go ahead' he grunted and with that, I headed out to do a couple of runs. A while later, I had my work done and it was time for me to go home, I was fairly tired at this stage after it being a difficult night with the snow and all that. Well, before I went any further, I decided to swing by the house where I left the two brothers, just check on them, in case they did not make it indoors. I drive by the porch and there was no sign of them, they must have got in, thank God, all is fine.

I drive on for about 20 yards and then I saw two people, one lying on top of the other, in the snow and the temperature still at the 17° freezing level. I got out of the car and the wind chill, it went right through me. I called out to them what were they doing. There was little or no response, so what was I to do. I tried to wake them up but they were out cold. I started to carry them on their homeward journey once again.

I soon found out that it was the wrong porch I took them to, they lived in the house. Since the resident brother was somewhat co-operating with me, I took him around the back of the house to where the entrance was. He gave me the set of keys that he had. To look at them, you'd swear that he was working as a doorman in Fort Knox, there was so many of them there.

After trying every key that he had, he eventually realized that he didn't live on this floor at all, no, it was the next floor up. By this time, I must have had the patience of Joab, I got him up the stairs, went through the keys one more time and managed to open the door. Once I got him inside, I went down and grabbed the other boyo, took him up the stairs and dumped him just inside the door.

I was a happy man after getting them home because, if I had not returned that night, there's no doubt, that those two would have died on account of the freezing temperatures. I have been thanked so many times over that one act and recently I was asked why did I return that night? Well, I just had not made sure that they had got in, you see, I always wait, whether man or women, for them to get inside the door. I know that some people don't want you to wait but if they are anyway under the influence of drink, I won't go until they're inside the door. Now, I must say that it very seldom happens that the person is not able to get in. There's often panic about the keys, are they lost, where did I leave them? etc., I usually tell them to check their pockets or look in their bag and that usually solves the problem. The right hand sometimes finds them in the left hand. All that panic for nothing, you know, it happens almost every night but that's life.

Drunks.

I have seen and heard most of what a drunk can do over the many years in dealing with them. The drunken man, if he is still able to talk, usually does not want to shut up. The reaction from the females is usually different, where silence is the preferred mode of operation. You can expect anything from the male, you could be complimented for your tolerance for listening or you could be abused for being just there to take them home. I know of a few characters who would be prime candidates for the 'drunk's hall of fame'. The contenders, well, there would be millions of them and everyone would have their own claim to fame.

I have heard of what they have done and of course what they are going to do, which is usually a repeat of what they have already done. After dropping them off, I have seen them attempt climbing trees, grab a tree and dance into a spin like as if they were on a carousel. They'd eventually let go and go spinning and hopefully toward the direction to where they are supposed to be going in the first place.

Other times there has been attempts made late at night to collect the mail out of an outside mail box. This has often proved to be too difficult to open, so as a last resort, I have seen them remove the mail box, complete with the post. It would be pulled up out of the front garden and taken inside for further examination. Gates at the entrance of houses have often been used as carousel rides and they would almost complete a circle, only to return back to the spot where they got on.

They would usually stay swinging back and forth on the gate until rescued and shown the entrance to their residence.

Life In The USA & Freedom.

Americans for the most part, know very little about Ireland. While you could understand them not knowing where Taughmaconnell or Innisvickalaun is, some of the Towns in Ireland have changed names. Usually, the ancestors would have come from Cork or Galway.

If they were asked if they were ever in Ireland, the normal answer would be no, however, for those of them who have been there, the usual answer would be Galway. "Do you know where you stayed in Galway?". "We stayed in balls of snow". I needed to give that answer more thought, maybe there was another Galway nearer to the North Pole with a B&B called "Balls Of Snow" or something like that. When they verified that it was the Galway in Ireland that they were talking about, it suddenly dawned to me what they were talking about – Ballinasloe !!!

Usually, their ancestors would have come from Ireland even though none of their names would reflect it. You'd have names the likes of Jamaal Murphy Thameski. I remember one day, I picked up a colored man and he soon recognized my accent and told me that he was Irish too. When I asked him what part of Ireland he came from, 'Dorchester', he said, and also, he was called after two kings that were in Ireland long ago. 'Don't you believe me?' he enquired, I replied, 'Well, I don't doubt you'.

He then produced his driving license, which clearly stated that his name was 'Jeffrey Fitzgerald Lynch'. He said 'Now, isn't that as Irish as you can get?' He then asked me, did I know of the Kings in Ireland and I said 'Yes, Fitzgerald was King in Dublin but the real King was Lynch, who hailed from Cork'.

I listen to things like that every year and some are crazier than others. I was once asked, 'did I drive to the USA?' 'No,' says I, 'I did not drive to the USA but I did do a bit of driving, since I arrived here'. Other people's questions would go as follows, 'Where is Ireland?' I replied 'It's the nearest country to the USA, across the Atlantic Ocean'. This particular Einstein replied back 'so it's near Arizona?' 'Close' says I.

Another time, I had two fellows in the taxi and they came out with a good one. One of them asked, was it very green in Ireland, I said Yes, we get a lot of rain, so the place is very green. The other fellow says, 'Well, I knew that', 'How did you know that' says the other Boyo, 'Sur, isn't it part of Greenland!'.

'Do you eat potatoes all the time in Ireland?' was asked. I answered, 'We eat them all right, but not for our breakfast, as is done in the USA'. 'Did you ever eat a Leprechaun?' 'Yes', says I, 'but only on very special occasions'.

The biggest surprise that the Americans get, when they first arrive in Ireland, is the freedom. They preach freedom to the rest of the world, not realizing that, they fall short of it big time themselves. America is a country that you cannot get a drink in a bar legally until you are 21 and after that you need ID to go into most places of entertainment.

When it snows, you have to, by law, clear out the snow in front of your house and clear it from around the fire hydrant. I read about an 85 year old man who was sent to jail because he did not clear the snow outside his home. Freedom means nothing, especially, if you have an outstanding fine for anything, maybe dropping a cigarette butt, fishing without a permit, a parking fine or anything at all. One false move and you are in trouble.

You will not be able to renew your driving license, remember, you cannot drive without a license. In fact, you could not even cash a check or gain entry to a night club or bar without that driving license. You might as well be in jail, only, nobody can visit you, unless they themselves are a resident or a US citizen. To visit someone in Jail, you yourself have to be checked out by the police which can take a week or more. After all that, you are then given approval for a 45 minutes visit, say 9.15 at night and the only choice you have is take it or leave it. If that is not suitable for you, you are told that this is a jail not a hotel.

The visit itself is not very pleasant, you cannot have anything on you and everything has to be stored in a locker. Your watch, keys, everything, even paper money will show up when you are scanned, and then you would be refused straight away. If you do manage to get access, you have to go through at least 3 sets of doors.

When a set of doors open, you step through, that door then closes and the next one opens up. This process continued until you reach the visiting area. You might finish up being seated outside a pane of glass, talking on a phone, just like death row as seen on the TV, the only difference is that the inmate in front of you is locked up for drinking or been disorderly or something minor like that. It certainly does not warrant the security measures that are dished out.

Some of the people that go to jail, for these minor offences, learn a tough lesson. Unfortunately, if one is picked up, there's very little they can do. They are allowed one phone call and you'd better get through to someone that can help you, because you could easily be left in jail for weeks or months on end without anyone knowing where you are and little or no help on the way.

There's nothing that I know of, that can be done for a person that gets into trouble or is arrested, say, at 5.30 on a Friday evening. It's going to be Monday Morning at least before there's a consulate office that is open and indeed, you could be told that it has to be a family member who needs to contact the consulate before anything will be done. No one seems to understand that they might not want their family to be involved, which is understandable, I suppose.

Late Night Runs.

While one would not want to know what was going on, the excuses often, do not make sense. When you have someone going out to pick up tickets for 'Disney on Ice' in June, at 3am in the morning, in an area where 'ice' means something totally different, you should be a little weary of those characters.

I have taken people to see 'Mother' at 2am, to pick up shirts or boots that were left there by mistake, earlier in the evening. When you see 'mother' at the door, who looks more like Bob Marley and your passenger looks a lot different, you might begin to wonder about the mother and son. But anyway, it's important to have a clean shirt and boots when you're going to work!. The excuses sometimes are just too much.

On time, I took a customer to her 'Granny' because they needed to collect some baby food that they left in the apartment earlier on. Granny, God bless her, looked great. I'd say, she wasn't a day over 25. Looking at her, you would think that she must have been a devout user of that 'Oil of Ulay' but one thing is certain, her grand-daughter was a devout user of something else. Whatever that something was, I doubt it if the 'Avon Lady' was the supplier!.

I had a fellow in the taxi one night and he was looking for some late night pep. He spotted a supplier on a small bike that provides an easy getaway by going down one way streets or going by blocked off streets if the need arises. Anyway, my passenger asked him if his name was Moses. He says 'No, I am not Moses'. 'You are Moses, I talked to you before', 'No, I am not Moses, leave me alone'. This banter continued on for a few moments and I then said that I was getting out of here, no more of this and I started to drive away. I was not driving long at the time and was not until a while later that I realized the dangers in getting involved in this kind of transaction.

Anyway, to get back to the story, my fare was not satisfied so he asked me, did I know the password that was needed to complete the transaction? 'No, I don't know what it is, and I never even knew you needed a password, I know nothing' says I. After a while, my fare got me to return again to where Moses was. This time, I told my fare that there would be no communications from the Taxi. I told him to get out of the car and talk to Moses across the street.

The conversation struck up again, 'You are Moses', 'No, I'm not', 'I know you are Moses', 'I am not Moses', 'Yes, you are Moses' 'Who sent you', 'Jesus sent me!'.

Apparently, that response clinched the deal, Moses asked him 'what can I get you', 'What have you got?' The response was 'Anything you want, man.'

Late Night Runs In The Rain.

On time, I was driving down the street on a very wet night, the rain was coming down in torrents and my passenger told me to stop the car. She let down the window and stuck the head out. There was no one to be seen on the street but anyway, she yells out 'Jason' and with that about six 'Jasons' appeared and some of those boyos were even dressed in short skirts and the like. The 'blond' Jason was dressed in the usually Miss Fit Clothes, red in color and in fact, he looked a bit like Santa, only it was a bit early for him, this was October.

The person in the car got out and went over to talk to Jason in the rain. They both returned to the car and asked me to wait for a couple of minutes. 'Two minutes', I said. Well in about the two minutes, Jason was back and she gets out of the car. One minute later, with a little haggling the business was done, everyone was happy. I had been paid $30 up front so I was ok. You always need to get the money first if your fare was going to an area that you might not be familiar with or in some cases, you are familiar with. Of course, if the passenger is returning to where you picked them up, get paid first, unless it's someone you know fairly well.

    I returned her back to where I first picked her up and then I went onto my next job. About five minutes later, the dispatcher called me and asked me where I was. 'The fare you dropped off a few minutes ago is looking for you', he told me. Back I went, she was waiting for me when I arrived, got into the car and told me to go back to the spot where we went before. 'I will kill Jason, I will kill him' she roared. I told her that going back would be a waste of time and money. 'Here's $30, just take me there' was her reply.

    Anyway, I did just that. When we arrived, she did the usual calling out for Jason. This time however, the response was a little bit different. After much roaring and ranting, the only creature to make any appearance on the street was a cat. Maybe, he was called Jason too but at this stage our 'blond' Jason was long gone. After a few minutes and a sore throat she asked me to take her back home again. 'I will kill him,' she said, 'he sold me powder for my face, instead of powder for my nose.

    I'm sure that it was just an honest mistake on Jason's part, I'm sure he went straight to the Church, praying for forgiveness at what had happened! In any case, I an absolutely sure that that 'mistake' probably cost my darling woman $300 or more, not to mention the $60 that ended up in my pocket. What a waste.

On another night, I was not long driving at the time and I had two men in the car. One of them got out and started talking to one of the locals. After a brief discussion, everything seemed fine, he returned to the car and asked me to take them to the convenience store. I drove there, one of them went in and came out two minutes later with two cans of coke.

They opened up the coke cans, emptied the drink out on the street and then our two 'craftsmen' went to work shaping the cans into two tubes. I knew right well what they were trying to do and unfortunately for the boys, I called a halt to their actions in the car and told them that they had to wait a while longer until we got back to their original destination.

Looking For Directions.

If you are looking for directions in any major USA city, well, best of luck to you. Some places where a lot of lost visitors finish up would have people holding signs saying '$5 for directions', however that is usually the extent of their command of the English language. The directions given are usually in Spanish or Vietnamese. You may as well give a bicycle to a fish rather that give those kinds of directions to a lad whose second language is Irish.

I remember one time, pulling into a gas/petrol station in Los Angles and of course, I was looking for directions. The man there said, 'I give you directions but I want two dollars for Pop who is in a wheelchair'. Like any decent West Of Ireland man would do, I give the two dollars and got my directions. As I pulled away I looked in my rear mirror and I was surprised to see what my two dollars had did, Pop arose from his wheelchair and walked over to a phone booth while my 'guide' took his place and sat down in the wheelchair.

Well, that happened probably ten years ago, now-a-days, you'd have no hope at all of getting directions. The new people working there at the gas stations or convenience stores have absolutely no idea of where they are. They all look like they came from Africa or Bombay and the only conclusion that I can come to is, that they jumped out of the airplanes and wherever they landed, that was their new place of work.

As long as they could operate a cash register and talk on their mobile phones, they were happy. It's common practice now to hear the person behind the register yakking away in a language that no one knows, except maybe someone in Bombay or Swaziland. Heaven help you, if you need anything other than cigarettes or scratch tickets.

People That Tell All.

There are many people out there that just want to tell you their problems and very often, the taxi is going to be their outlet. The only thing you can do is listen, however, you are probably hoping for a green light to help you to speed up the journey but getting all red lights, just prolongs the agony. But sure what harm, that little problem of red lights and stops may well be small trouble in comparison to what your passenger might be going through.

The suicide story is always a difficult subject. 'Nobody cares for me' is the usual complaint and I really don't know what to say but I always try to reassure them by saying that it may seem that way but there are always people out there that care for you. 'I am going to end it all, I tell you and I want you to tell such a one when I am gone.' I've heard them say. I always say 'don't tell me anything like that' because you might be told something that could put them under more pressure to carry out their threat.

'I was never loved by my parents usually not though when I was leaving. I tried to hug my father and say goodbye. All he said was "don't do that". Those moments when parting from home can have a lasting effect on your life. In Ireland, we were never told we were loved, well it was not the way things were done in the sixties and seventies. The older people had a problem with showing their feelings and that was just the way it was.

Even to this day, I have been told many things by people that have a problem and I will not be writing about it in this book. Sometimes a person will say, 'I telling you this and I am not telling anybody else but when I am dead, tell such a one, this or that' I always reply it's not a good idea telling me because I cannot guarantee that I will not be gone before you.

No one knows when, where or how the end will come and after hearing this kind of stuff from people for the last few years, I was thinking that there should be kind of service available for people that want to leave a message, after their passing.

There must be thousands of people out there that want to say something or another to someone after their death. Whether it's 'I love you' or I have a secret bank account and here's the number or 'I have no money and you always said I was a millionaire, but the truth is I was no millionaire'. The message could be anything, a confession, a love affair, admitting to a crime, if a person wants to leave a message to someone after their passing, please do so but don't leave the message to a stranger.

To this end, I have now set up a service myself to cater for those people, it's available through the Internet at www.speakafterdeath.com.

This is a secure service and any messages that are entered are stored away and can only be accessed through a password. That password is the only way to gain access to the information and you can change the information as often as you'd like while you are alive. However, after your passing, the people that you left the messages for, would then be notified of any messages left for them. Further information is available on the web site.

Permits.

Now-a-days, you need a permit for almost everything you do around the home. Anything to do with the roof, any alterations inside or outside, it's a money racket. You have to provide them with information like, the price that the work will cost, when it starts, when it will be finished, then and only then, you will be then given the permit and of course you have to pay for that too. Recently there was what was called a 'sting operation' against householders that might be carrying out work without the proper permits.

City officials would park outside 'Do It Yourself' suppliers and watch those people put timber, plaster, paints or anything that could be used for home improvements in their cars or trucks. They then took the number of the vehicle and checked it against the address and afterwards watched that house or apartment to see what trash was being put out. The city would then send a bill for the work that was carried out. Freedom is just another word.

There was this gas station I knew and visited often. They used to be always selling Twix bars and chewing gum and one night, those items were all missing. I thought that they were sold out but what had happened was that an official had told them that they were fined because they did not have a permit to sell them.

How about this one, the bars that sells tea and coffee, needs to have a permit in order to provide milk. Permits, permits, law, law, it's all a racket.

Opening A Business.

This will certainly entertain you, it's on live TV, you appear before a five or six people panel that has been elected by God only knows who and they have held that position for years. They are from the Health Environment Historic Society and you have to go before them with your lawyer to try and make a case for yourself to open a business. Now, this is open to the public and you can be sure there will be plenty of people there to object to you, no matter what you are trying to do. The only thing that there's no objecting to now-a-days are hairstylists, nails salons and Chinese restaurants.

You will be questioned on your experience in the business and why you want to set up at that location. Now, the chairman of this meeting is always very nice and you could easily get the impression that he wants to help you, only to find out that when it comes to a vote, he will always join the rest and you are left wondering what just happened. This same meeting deals with bars and restaurants and if you need to get an extra table or chairs, you need their permission. If you need to change your staff, you need to appear before the band to get their approval, once again, freedom is just another word.

I remember someone appearing one time before them looking for permission to operate a karaoke bar, you would think you he asked them questions about life in one of the stars in the next solar system. I don't know where they have been but none of them had ever heard of karaoke. After a lot of discussion, it was decided that they would go to a karaoke bar and see for themselves, what it was like.

Off they went, followed by the press and media, they were not really that impressed but they admitted that they might not be as well up in what's happening out there late at night. They all said that, they never go out after 9 o'clock, early to bed and early to rise seems to be their way forward, it certainly is not 'Just Go Do It'.

Quick Marriage.

I was told a story one night from a man that came to the USA in the Seventies. I don't think things happen as fast now, well, the marrying bit would not be as fast anyway. He arrived in the Seventies and he was in his early twenties. Coming from the country, he was used to going to a dance hall, enter the scrum and hope to get a dance from someone. Usually, all you got then was, to hear the music of the likes of Big Tom or some other band.

After finding his way around and getting started on a job, he started to go out to the bar. He was very surprised by the attention he was getting from a young American lady. She said, she always wanted an Irish man (she loved the brogue) and of course, her ancestors came here, from the highlands of Ireland, during the potato famine. This was her dream come true and no doubt, a lot of dreams for him as well.

After the night of chat, she invited him back to her apartment, things were moving fast, what could and would take months, if not years back in Ireland was happening right now in a matter of hours. The invitation to the bed was extended to him and while he had no experience what so ever, it was what he had dreamed of and also, it was high time he learnt something new.

Thinking of all the crazy nights back home, listening to 'four country roads' and singing it on the way home was now being forgotten, this was the way to go. Jane Doe was going to change it all. Since Jane Doe had a lot more experience than John Doe, she led the way and got things moving. 'This is awesome', Jane was saying. 'I can see Ireland, let's go, let's go. I can see Leprechauns, this is awesome.' After a short time, things were coming to a peak and after some more Leprechauns sightings, the two seconds of magic happens. Jane Doe screamed 'marry me, marry me'.

In that fleeting moment of madness, weakness, lust or whatever you'd call it, John Doe who had transferred command of the thinking process from his brain to some other bodily organ, shouted out, 'Yes, I will marry you'. Early next morning, he was marched down to the City Hall to get a marriage license and he was married a week later. This whirlwind marriage occurred two weeks after he arrived in the USA and it would, no doubt, take some explaining things to the folks back home.

Phone calls to Ireland at that time, were not that common as very few homes had phones and letters was really the only method of communication. With all the excitement about the marriage, and that things were going very well, he wanted to let the family know back home what was happening. This was to be the second letter. The first letter hadn't even arrived home yet, and in that he wrote, 'I arrived, place is big here. I don't know yet how long I will stay, write to you soon'. This new letter was going to be a beauty. In it, he would have to detail, what life was like in America and work in somehow that he now had a wife. He started off by writing 'things are very good here, I have lots of work and I just got married last week. We are very happy, I will tell you more as time goes by but rest assured, everything is good right now.

With the letter completed, off he went to the post office to post it. He was thinking in his own mind that they would be surprised at the news but since it was good news, they'd be fine. He was looking forward to hearing their reply and of course, how the news went down with the neighbors.

A few days after the letter was mailed out, John Doe arrived home and found Jane Doe missing, he looks around and saw that almost everything of hers was gone. He waited that afternoon, that night, the following day, the following week afterwards but still no sign of the Wife. He didn't know anyone who knew her and the two witnesses at the wedding ceremony were strangers so it eventually sunk in that she was gone for good. Around this time, he was thinking that the letter would have been delivered and he was hoping against hope that the letter would have gotten lost or something. That was a long shot and he was bracing himself for the reply letter.

About a month later, that dreaded arrived. He was thinking that he would have been banished from the family at this stage and that he would no longer be welcome home. The letter started by saying, glad to hear you are getting on well, everything is fine here. The black cow had a black calf, the sheep are now in the big field and we sowed the potatoes without you this year. You will probably be home to eat them.' It continued 'stop wasting your time, writing jokes to us here about being marrying. You were always a joker. It's time to grow up, now that you are so far away and try to be more sensible when you are writing to us. That's all for now, write to us when you have some news'.

Jane Doe never came back, nor did he find out where she went. He never got married since, well, marriage is supposed to be 'until death do us part' and he does not know that part of it yet.

See Who.

On a late night call to a Chinese restaurant, I encountered the following, I suppose, not being able to speak Chinese did not help me either. I got a pick-up call to go to a Chinese restaurant and when I got there, it appeared to be closed, anyway I go inside and I was greeted with 'closed, closed'. I replied 'I am taxi driver', 'closed' he said. I replied again 'I am taxi driver, you need taxi?'. The conversation continued 'No, I am taxi driver'. 'You for see?' 'Who see, I am taxi driver,' 'Yes, taxi driver for see who'.

Now, after a twelve hour shift, you would ask yourself, what am I doing here and what had just happened. I decided to get out of there and I got into my car and pulled away. Shortly afterwards, I hear the dispatcher calling 'how did you do with the Chinese job?'. I told him that I didn't do anything because they did not understand me. 'There's a language problem with them' I said, 'they only understand numbers there'.

The dispatcher told me that the Chinaman was on the phone and he says that he is running after you. I looked in rear view mirror and sure enough, there's a Chinese man, running after me. I stopped, he gets in and says 'see you, go away you are for me, see who, I am see who'. Oh yes, I see you now.

Singing In A Cab.

Singing in a cab can start at anytime, you'll never know when it's going to start or what classic you are going to hear. I have heard the full range of songs and some I will try and recall. After a football match, you might have, You are my Larsson, You keep me happy scoring goals.... Alan Shearer. You are my Larsson, you keep me happy scoring goals, were off to Dublin in the Green in the Green and then onto Queen, these two usually go together. How many times have I heard 'The Fields of Athenry', especially for this cab driver? Hundreds of times.

The Banks of my own Lovely Lee would be recited from the Cork choir. Slievemon would be lamented from the Tipperary Singers, The Offaly Rover by the Farmer's Choir. With two singers in the back, usually one would be trying to be louder than the other. One singing, the Flower of Scotland while the other would try to sing Dublin in the Rare Old Times. try mixing that sometime with the comments when they finish, when will we ever learn?

By far, the most popular song in the taxi has always been 'the streets of New York', whether it's the yellow taxi that inspires them or something else. It's always nice to hear that song, whether it's sung by someone under the influence of alcohol or the beautiful version sung by Colette from Galway and Julie from Cork, that stand out in my mind.

Snow & The Wrong House.

I always ask, 'where are you going?', the usual answer is, 'home'. I learned, a long time ago, that you could be taking someone for a long time to one place, only to find out that, they don't live there at all. A crystal ball would sometimes be very handy in those cases.

Some years back, I used to take a man home from the bar, a couple of times a week. I would nearly always be called for him as I knew where he lived and I was about the only one that was able to get him home safely. One snowy night, I was called to pick him up. Now this particular night, he was very drunk and not very cooperative, however I drove him to his residence, well, the place that I had taken him for the last couple of years. I got him out of the car but he fell down in the snow. I got him up but he fell down again shortly afterwards. I then had to drag him up the steps of the house, got his keys, tried opening the door with every key that he had, tried all the keys again but no good, rang the bell, no response.

He was sitting on the porch in the snow when he says to me 'what are you doing?', I told him that I was trying to get him in the door, 'what door?' he says, I said 'you're home now'. He says 'I am not home, I don't live here anymore, get me out of here, my wife lives here now'. I must say, it was easier to move him away from the house, than to get him up the steps, in the first place. After all that, I finally got him home. He did not live far from his old residence and had only moved in there a week or two before. So since that episode, I always ask people where they live and sometimes I am asked 'how many times have you taken me there before, don't you remember?'

The Airport Taxi Job.

Driving, while most of the time the police give taxis a break, unless you are just very blatant or aggressive, sometimes, you might be stopped for running a red light or not fully stopping at a stop sign, the best thing is to say nothing when stopped. Saying that you are sorry does not mean anything, no need to be sorry, you will be told to stop talking or else the ticket will get bigger if you don't stop talking.

I was once trying to drop off a person at Terminal E, the Aer Lingus terminal in Logan Airport, it was someone going back to Ireland. There were cars parked everywhere and I had already driven around twice and just could not find a place to stop and drop them off. In desperation, I stopped just to drop the person off but as soon as I stopped, there was a hard knock on the window, a state trooper. Now, you definitely don't say anything to them, at the best of times they are just not talkative, the ones that are at the airport are usually there on disciplinary matters for something they have done at some other place. So usually, you need God's help when you come to their attention.

'License and registration' he demanded 'take care of your fare'. Trooper, 'How long have you been driving a cab?' 'Three months I answer'. 'Three months, your nose is getting long!' Nothing but silence from me. The trooper then asked me how many times had I come to the Airport. I told him that this was my first time trooper. 'Your nose is getting longer'. 'Sorry' I said, 'trooper, I don't understand you'. 'Well, you know what happened to Pinocchio, when he told lies, his nose got longer and yours is very long right now". I said 'sorry trooper, I don't understand you, I am from Ireland and I have never heard of Pinocchio'. The Trooper said 'take those documents and get to hell out of here'.

That will go down as one of the great escape of the time because you just don't get away with anything at the airport.

Taxi Driving.

Driving a cab can be best described as an adventure into the unknown.
To many, it's not really a job, you are just sitting there in a car, no work involved, then of course, to others, you are not working unless you are breaking rocks. I have been called by many names while I have been driving and some of the most common and notable ones are, the Captain, Galway Mick, Handball Mick, the Irish Driver. I have had lots of compliments from many nice people and I want to thank you all.

I have often been asked, why do you drive a cab, because it's not a job many of the Irish do in the USA. I seem to be the only one from Ireland driving a taxi around the Quincy area for the last ten years I am often asked what else do I do for work or do I do this for fun or is it a hobby. Ask any cab driver about the fun part of the job, after closing time in the bars.

I learned a long time ago, not to be in any hurry when picking up passengers at a bar because, if you are in a hurry, you're probably the only one. You'll just finish up waiting because that person could have made a lot of new friends in that bar while he was there. Every one of those new friends will have to be notified of his departure and arrangements then made to meet again, probably the next day or night. It's important not to rush out and even people check the stools where their friends were sitting, just in case they would have fallen down and it would not be right to leave without saying goodbye.

Now that you have your passenger finally in the car, you need to prepare yourself for anything, you could be told 'sorry for delaying you but sure you're not busy anyway you were in no rush to get me out'. Well, there is often a rush to get them home, you pray for green lights to minimize the time you have to listen to whatever is been said.

I always remember the words of an old man in Ireland that went 'drink can make a fool out of a wise man' now, that was a smart man. I have often said that to people and they ask me 'why didn't he say something about women?' Well, at that time, that old man, in his wildest dreams, would not have imagined a women getting drunk. Back then, he said, his now famous words 'the only place a woman went or was seen was at Mass on a Sunday'.

Sometimes someone that is drunk can be difficult to handle, but things usually work out, if you give it a little extra time. The most important thing to know is where they are going. However, getting that information can be difficult at times. Sometimes, it would be easier to get the home address of an FBI agent. A phone number is often a great help too, you would make an attempt at calling the wife or a girlfriend on the phone and then his lordship usually responds immediately with 'don't do that'.

The person that has just arrived in the States can be the most difficult because they usually don't know much about where they are. They're maybe on holidays and could be looking for someplace like South Park or Mayfield in Ireland but they are in the wrong country.

'Take us to the Holy Grail' I've been asked. I'd reply with 'I don't know where that is, how about the Holy Ground, would that be right? 'as long as it sells drink, it will do!'

Two middle aged men from Ireland were looking for 'The Cattle Mart' they told me that they sell everything there. 'Well, I don't know about that' I said, 'it would be mainly cattle and I don't know of any around here, you might have to go to Texas for a cattle mart'. 'No, there's one near here somewhere. Good prices on clothes and everything' they replied. I just then realized that instead of the Cattle Mart, they were looking for Walmart!.

The record number of times I had to go to a bar to pick up any one person is seven. I still did not manage to get him and the next day, when I saw him I told him that I had called seven times to collect him the night before. He replied, 'you would have thought that, after three or four times, you have realized that I was not going and left me alone, it's time you copped yourself on'.

When called to a bar to pick someone up and they are not ready to go, it's usually not a problem because most likely, someone else will jump at the chance to go somewhere and if not, it's no big deal. I was always well paid for going back for them later.

On very rare occasions, when drink does the talking and somebody just does not want to go home, you might get 'I am not going to pay you'. I always say 'no problem, I will get you home' and that is usually the end of that conversation until you reach their destination, and then it's 'how much is it?'

If I was to drive for another two years without being paid, I still would be owed nothing by the Irish people because they have overpaid me for every trip that I have taken them on, over the past number of years. Most of my trips are local or into downtown Boston, however, my longest trip ever was from Quincy to New York. It happened when four young

Irish wanted to go to a late night bar and since New York has plenty of them, that was the place they wanted to go. The trip would take four hours and the fair was $475. To radio was not working in the car and they sang all the way down. I heard the reason Billy Reid had to die at least thirty times and many more such songs but we made it there safely and they paid me very well. They did not call me to come back, the Greyhound Bus took care of that.

The drunk sitting behind you in the car would tell you how much he admires you and he would drive, only he is too smart to drive. He says 'how do you listen to so many drunks' and 'everyone admires you for your patience' and he goes on 'how much rubbish (or maybe another word) have you heard, in your years driving'. If I had made use of all the rubbish that was fed to me, I would now be the proud owner of a six lane toll road to Ireland, with a few towns and cities thrown in as well. That's the amount of rubbish that I've heard.

Having listened to so much talk over the years, it may surprise you to know that, I cannot remember any of it. I am about 99% deaf to almost all of the conversations and I when it comes to my taxi passengers, what goes in one ear, goes out the other. Anyway, I like to mind my own business and why, in the name of God, would I want to remember anybody else's. About 80% of my business is dealing with the Irish community and I don't run into any problems with them.

No one ever knows what awaits you, the next stranger could be your last fare. You sometimes have the superman type character who has done it all. He has robbed, murdered, done 25 years in jail and he is just out and misses all his other life long friends in jail. He wants to get back to where he belongs, jail. Then he says that you talk like you just got off the boat.

I arrived here over 30 years ago and by plane. 'Well, how come you talk like Mrs. Doubtfire?', that's because I don't listen to anyone, here is the part that the 99% deafness works, very well. You usually part company with him after he pays his fare and is farewell words are 'I should have been home two hours ago, she is going to kill me for being late again'. I would often reply by saying that she could be sleeping.

'She never sleeps with both eyes closed, there's always one open and that is linked to the tongue' I've been known to pick up what appeared to be brave men but by the time they have reached their "Home Sweet Home", they are transformed into what appears to be a changed person.

Now how much of either they are, I don't know nor do I want to know, you just get paid in dollars, all other barter is not accepted. They would often bless themselves and look up to Heaven before entering "Home Sweet Home"

Elvis.

A good many years ago, it was a wet and windy night and I picked up a fare outside the Train Station. A man gets in and tells me to take him to an Oldies club in the next town. I took him there and he was listening to his music on his headset, since no conversation was taking place in the car. It is difficult driving at night in the rain because the conditions would require my full attention. When we got to the destination, he asked, how much the fare was. I told him that it was $10 and the man paid me. I took a good look at him as he was getting out of the car and there he was, Elvis. I had just seen Elvis.

Later on, I was saddened when I found out he died. There are now about 20,000 new Elvis's around the place, so it's possible, I picked up one of them but something tells me, in the back of my mind, that the fair that I had that wet and rainy night was the man himself, the King.

Another time, I picked up supermen after a concert. This fellow was on a high, you know, the ones that can take on the world, in there own mind. Anyway, he told me to take him downtown. When I told him that I would, he recognized my accent and said 'Oh, you are from the old country' 'Yes' I replied, 'Were you at the concert?' he asks. I told him that I wasn't since I was working. He asked me then, 'Why are you in this country?' and I replied by saying, 'I often use the words that Sir Edmund Hilary used when asked 'why did you climb Mount Everest?' The answer was 'because it was there' and that is why I am in the USA, because it's there. I want to be here, well, some of the time, anyway. I am leaving tomorrow for Ireland, are you going to come with me?' 'I am not ready to leave that fast' says I. 'Why aren't you? I am going tomorrow and I am going to get everyone of those British invaders, out of Northern Ireland.'

Apparently, he was just come out from a Wolfe Tone's concert where he had gotten a briefing on Irish History and the cause of all her troubles. Those British invaders had a lot to pay for and he was the man to do the job. That was a few years ago now and I have had no feedback on how he got on, but I am sure he is still getting counseling at those concerts on what needs to be done.

Taxi Offers.

As most of my work is dealing with the Irish, I just do my job and get paid for it. Anyway, when you reach a certain age, you should realize that the only thing anyone wants from you, is to pick them up and drop them off safely. I am often told, mostly by younger drivers of the many offers, that are made to them. As for myself, the offers now-a-days are few and far between. It can happen that some nice young lady might say that her mother is coming out for a week or two and she would be tired of looking after her and since she always wanted to fix her up for a night, maybe I would take her out for something to eat. 'It would save me from cooking for a night' she added. And for me, that's a no go.

I remember getting the call one night over the radio for a pick up. I get there and this lady, we'll say she was in her 50+ years, said to me to take her to Boston and that she would be coming back straight away again. With this, alarm bells go off straight away, 'I will need money up front' I said. 'I always look after the drivers was the reply'.

Remembering other great offers that I would have refused in the past, I said 'that's no good to me, I need money, at least $30'. She replied, 'I will take care of you, whatever you want'. 'I want $30 for a start', says I. 'No, no, I don't have that kind of money, would you like a threesome?' 'No' says I, '$30, that's all I want'. She replied back 'I have one last offer to you and it's the best I can do. How's about a mother and daughter threesome?' 'No, no.' says I, 'What would your daughter think of her mother doing such a thing, its disgraceful behavior and it certainly makes little of your daughter'.

She replied, 'No, I am not making little of the daughter, I **am** the daughter'. I shouted 'just get out and leave me alone'. Her parting shot was 'Just my luck. I must have gotten the only married taxi driver in Boston'.

Tour Of Boston.

For those people who are visitors to Boston, there are thousands who are often disappointed by what's on offer. If you were not on a bar hopping holiday, you could indeed run out of places to visit very quickly. JFK library is an interesting place to go but it would not be for everyone. The science museum, well, that would be a must for everyone. As regards the cheers bar, that would come under bars so don't expect too much.

Then you have the Red Sox baseball game. Now, if you want to see grown men that are paid thousands of times too much, for swinging a baseball bat and hitting a ball and then watch other grown men try to catch it, you are in for a treat. When they eventually hit the ball but they usually have many attempts at striking it, before that happens.

Now, if you were unlucky enough to get to a game and it rains, those highly paid men don't play but you the spectator, who might have paid over a hundred dollars for a ticket, will have to sit in the rain for maybe up to four hours before the game is called off. That's a nice way to spend your holiday.
If you have watched Jamsie O' Connor, DJ Carey or any other fine hurler in action, you would be disappointed with Pedro and company, getting millions for swinging the bat.

Another great outing that you should give a bit of thought to because you would have seen a half hour promotional video of it on the flight over to Boston is the Duck Tour. This tour is on a bus that converts over to a boat to travel on the water. Now, I don't know when the promotional video was shot, but it's a lot different now than it was when you take the trip. When you take this trip, you'll see downtown Boston, which is always under construction with the Big Dig. This has been going on for years and every so often, new sections are opened up and that only disrupts the traffic even more.

As I've said before, the 14 Billion that has been spent would have been put to better use in building another city outside Boston. Then, you would not have the inconvenience that has been caused by his Big Dig. Of course, the tour around the Big Dig would include many more construction sites with large holes dug in the ground, which you might think would be the new Grand Canyon but they eventually will be filled with concrete containing new offices and shops with names like Tommie Hilfiger, or Diesel. Also on your tour, you will see an endless amount of wooden boardings of many different colors covered with poster advertising. This is a tour that no visitor is ever going to forget. By right, they should call it, the Muck Tour.

Where Do You Live? Schull.

I pick up passengers a lot of the time outside Irish bars. I learned a long time, not to ask where they live because the answer was as always the same, home. One needs a little more information, especially late at night because there's no guarantee that even they know where they are going.

One night I pick up two men and I asked them 'where do you live?. 'Schull, Co. Cork' was the answer! Now, I was in the Dorchester area of Boston, I asked them what part of Boston were they staying in but they replied that a man in the bar said that the taxi driver would know. I told them that I would need some address, they continued to give me further information, they informed me that they were staying beside a burned out house. I then asked them how long have they been in this country and they told me, 6 hours. I immediately returned to the bar to see the man that said the taxi driver would know, thankfully, he had an address so I got them home safely.

People often come to America with an address that they got from someone in a pub in Ireland, a year or two before. They come out here not realizing that things change, people move on and its very difficult to start looking for a place to stay. It's big money for a motel room and apartments are usually not furnished and with a payment of 1st. and last month rent, plus a deposit, it's usually well out of most peoples personal finances.

Best Wife In The World.

Believe it or not, but when most men are drunk, they actually praise their Wives. 'My wife is the best in the world, eighteen years married. I'd do it all again, she's a great woman, she is angry with me now but that's ok.' This particular lad continued on, 'She is angry with me because I cannot find her car. I had it and I left it somewhere, I don't know where, I am looking all around everyday for it, the search will continue until I find it. I am also looking for my truck, I don't know where that is, I left it at a bar a couple of weeks ago and I need it. She is a great woman. She threw me out at 4am this morning, it's not the car she was giving out about, it's the driveway at the house. I was to put in a new one but I cannot find my truck to do the job. it's all ripped up and she wants it fixed.'

He goes on, 'She's a great woman, 18 years married and I am very happy with her.' I took him to his home and yes, the driveway did look like ground zero, loads of bricks and rubbish thrown everywhere. He keeps going on, 'She says that I am the biggest B*****x that ever came to this country, I don't know where she is going to park the car, if it is found' Ah, married bliss!

Look Out For My Cat.

I picked up a fare late one night and he told me to take him to Randolph. This would be around a twelve or thirteen dollar fare at the time. 'Watch out for my cat,' he says, 'the cat will be waiting for me'. He then gives me $20 and told me to get him home safely. I was driving along the route that I would always go in order to get to that destination and I was about to bear right at a junction when he says 'stay left'.

This meant that I was going away from the direction that I would normally go, but sure maybe, he knew a shorter way. I kept going and I had not gone too far when he says, 'you are going the wrong way'. I said that 'this is the way you wanted me to go'. He said, 'Sorry, I know I did' and he gives me another $20. 'Just get me home to my cat' he said. I turned back and went the way I should have gone in the first place.

At this stage, I had gotten $40 which was much more than the fare would ever be. He told me that he was a heron choker. 'Did you ever hear that before?' he asked, 'Yes, I did' I replied. 'I am from Canada', he says and he gave me another $20. The total now was $60 which was far too much and we even haven't reached the destination yet.

He says 'look out for my cat, it will be waiting for me'. I arrived and sure enough, the cat was sitting there waiting for the heron choker.

He asked me how much did he owe me and I told him that he didn't owe me anything. Then he says 'take this'. Another $14 was handed over and that would have probably been the right amount to start with!.

He then says 'I would give you more, if I had more but that's all I have on me now'. I said, 'No, you have given me more than enough'. 'But I would like to give you more, just wait there for a moment'. Now it was decision time for me, I had already gotten $74 for my effort and in my mind I was thinking 'what was he going to come out with, maybe a gun'.

I waited for a little while longer and sure enough, he came back out and gave me another $100 and says, 'that's for getting me home to my cat'.

I wish everybody loved their naughty cat as much!

You Talk Like My Father.

I picked up fare at the train station on time, he was a man in his mid-twenties. He told me where he wanted to go and when I answered him, he says 'you talk like my father, you must be from Tipperary'. I said 'no, but I'm not that far from it. He said, 'my father is from Tipperary'. I said 'I bet he has a Hurley' but he replied back that he didn't. I thought that to be strange but the conversation continued anyway. He then said, 'but I am going to get one, and I am going to travel with it'. I said 'I expect your first stop will be Canton'.

Now, for those of you not in the know, Canton is the centre for all the GAA activities, football, hurling and so on and it has probably the best facilities for Irish Games on the East Coast of America. 'I will be going all over the USA' he says. In my own mind, I was thinking maybe this character would be the new St. Patrick, teaching the game of hurling to people all over the states, displaying the skills in far away places and then he says 'I will be taking it to Tipperary'.

'Well', I said, 'there would be plenty of hurleys already there so there's no need to take yours'. He said 'they won't be like mine, I am saving a hundred dollars a week right now for it and in three years time, I'll be well on my way. My Hurley is going to be gold winged.
I was thinking that even D.J. Carey does not have anything like that. He then told me 'I will have, what my father never had, a Harley Davison'.

It was then I realised that we went slightly off track in the conversation. Two different ways of thinking but no harm done and we both got to where we wanted to go. I must get my hearing checked sometime.

Car Hire.

Now this is something for which you need to have your wits about you or else be prepared to pay whatever that bottom line says when you get the credit card bill. One time, I arrived in Orlando, Florida and it was a busy week for some reason or other, spring break or bike week, whatever. I had a booking for a car for two weeks and the pick up was in Orlando and I would then drop it off in Miami at a rate of $139 per week.

After queuing for an hour, I finally got to the counter where I was greeted by, 'my name is Brendan, I hope you are having a nice day because from now on, it's only going to get better'. Now, I knew everyone would be Brendan's lawful prey and I was going to be on my guard. He says 'Don't I have a great deal for you today. First time in Orlando?' he asked me. 'No, I've been here before. I have a car booked.' 'What's the name?' he asked. 'I don't see anything here for you, but not to worry, we can work this out'.

I was searching for the car booking reference number, which I found, Brendan did not seem too worried that I had found it. 'You got a great deal at $139 per week, however, I am going to make that better for you, I am going to give you a red convertible soft top, hard top, all the works, for just $14 extra per day, a total of only $196 on top of your $278, isn't that a awesome deal or what?'.

'I don't think so', says I, so he went away for a couple of minutes and when he returned he said something like that today was his birthday and that he was 26 and he felt real good that he was able to give me a convertible for only $7 per day so 'how about that? Think of the impression you are going to make driving that car'.

'None' was my answer to that, I said, 'No, no, no, just give me the car I have booked at $139 per week'. He goes away again for another few minutes. When he returned, he said, 'I told you its my birthday today, 26, I feel so good that I am going to give you the convertible because you came a long way and you deserve it.

Now the reason for Brendan's generosity was that, he had only this type of cars left and as it was evening and he was finishing off his shift, he let me have the red convertible. After a few days, I worked out the 007 top and headed down the Florida Keys. Returning to Miami two weeks later, I had some time to spare and as it's usually a rush to the plane, you are told to put the keys in a special envelope, drop them in a box and everything will be taken care of by the amigo with your credit card.

With the time to spare, I took the keys and the paper work to the counter where man thanked me and told me that everything was ok and that my credit card would take care of everything. I said 'Yes, how much is the total?'. 'Total?' he says, 'I don't know'. 'Well, I want to know, ok?' says I. He replied, 'I will have to get a senior consultant to make this out, are you in a rush?' 'No' says I, 'I have plenty of time to spare'. After about 10 minutes, the senior consultant came back to me and said the total was $469.

Now the amount should be $278 plus taxes, which is certainly less than the $200, as the credit card was covering the insurance. I said that the amount was wrong but he said no, the amount was right. I said, I had a car for $139 per week, he said, no, I had a car for $139 for one week and it was $330 for the second week.

I had signed for it and that was that. I said no, no. He said you signed for it right here, nothing that can be done. I said to call Orlando and he said no, we rent out over 500 cars a day in Orlando and there's no way of knowing who rented it to you. I said, his name was Brendan and it was his birthday on the day that I hired it. He just said, it's Brendan's birthday everyday.

I did not leave there until it was sorted out. They eventually called Orlando and got a new hire contract issued and I got the car for the $278 plus taxes. Now, if you were in the usually hurry back to catch your flight, what happens? You pay for Brendan's birthday, every day.

I know that this would never happen in Ireland. In all my years dealing with car hire people, I have always gotten a great deal, whether at Budget, Eyre Sq, Adrian or Noel have always looked after everyone at Shannon, Declan Colleran at Hertz, all gentlemen.

Renting A Car Without Directions.

I have written about the perils or renting a car but a new one happened to me recently. I arrived at Logan Airport and decided I would rent a car for a couple of days. Now at every airport up to that, you always see car hire booths with all the usual names there in front of you. This is not the case in Logan, these booths have now been replaced with phones and each car hire company has a free phone so all you have to do is lift up any phone and you have the car hire company on the other end. I lifted the phone and yes, contact was made straight away, I wanted a car for three days, no problem, your first name Michael, Michael Logan,

'No, Michael is my first name, Logan is where I am'. 'So your name is not Logan?' 'No, I am at Logan Airport, Boston Mass,' 'What can I get you?' 'A car for three days' I said, 'mid size will do,' and I gave them my credit card number and the amount was ok.' Where do I get the car?' I asked, 'I don't know', was the reply, 'you don't know where the car is, that I have hired?' 'No, I don't know, just go outside the building and a bus will pick you up and take you to a compound where your car will be waiting for you.

'Is it far away from here?' I asked, 'I don't know was the reply'. 'Will you be there for me to pick up the car?', 'No', was the answer, 'where are you?, I asked. 'I am in Bombay' was the reply.

Bombay where India is? You would have quite a bit of fun asking him about the traffic around the Big Dig, so be careful with those 1800 numbers, you could be getting through to anywhere in the world.

Driving.

A song in Ireland many years ago had the words 'if you survive through a crash on the highway, it's a miracle you are still here today'. Well, that is true because driving anywhere today can be best described as the survival of the fittest massive size trucks, buses, tankers carrying gas or dangerous chemicals and they all traveling at high speeds.

Just get out of their way, because if you are hit by one of these trucks, you'd better have your affairs in order because you most likely will be gone to the next life. Now, if you can survive these hazards, you have lots more to look out for, particularly the young drivers and indeed sometime the older one as well. The teenage girls are not to be ignored either, she usually knows how to drive straight ahead at high speed, smokes, listens to rap music and talk on mobile phones and all while learning how to drive.

The young male will think that he is invincible, no matter where he is in the world. He has it in his mind that he is the World's best driver and lover, so how can he be wrong. The probability is that, he's not the best at either but nevertheless, that myth can last for years and sometimes all though his life.

Then, you have the jeep and small trucks, the muscle men drive. Their motto is, 'Move over the rest of you drivers, you are a waste of my space'. The only comfort is that the law will always catch up with them and they are all potential customers for a cab, sooner, rather than later. When you do have them in the cab, they are still driving, even when they are in the back seat. Now and again, you get a comment, usually not very complimentary, 'I would have gone through that light, if I was driving' and 'why aren't you driving?' I'd ask, 'I lost my license' would be the answer. 'Oh, so you want me to lose mine as well.' 'Not really, I won't be looking for you to drive me away, if I am robbing a bank'. Well, that's good news.

There's a story that I'd like to tell you, about the old man driving around, looking for a place to park his Rolls Royce. After a long search, he finally sees a place and drives by it in order to reverse in, which would be the right way to park the car. As he goes into reverse, he sees that a small sports car in that same parking space that he was about to park in. He gets out of his Rolls and asked the driver of the sports car, 'did you see me indicate that I was going to park there?'

The driver of the sports car says, 'you are too slow, when you are young and nippy, you don't need much time to park you just drive. Don't waste time surveying where you're going to park, just park and get on with your life'. The old man gets back into his rolls and reverses into the little sports car, crushing it against the curb. The young nippy driver screamed, 'my beautiful sports car, what have you done, you have destroyed my car, are you mad?'

The old man gets out of his car and says, 'when your young and nippy, you can park anywhere but when your old and rich, you can push little sports cars out of the way!'

Fast Food Ordering.

Sometimes, ordering fast food can be a problem, all you see are people working there who are programmed to hear phrases like burger, cheeseburger, number 2, number 3 or whatever numbers that are available. I remember many years ago, when I was in a drive through, I got the usual 'how are you today? Today's special is a double cheeseburger with large fries and your choice of drink, all for $3.99.' I replied, 'Your geese are eating our potatoes'. The only question to be asked would be, what kind of drink would you like with that order?

Ordering fast food at night can be a problem especially if you are from Donegal, Derry, Belfast, Cork or Kerry. There's going to be a problem because, the person taking the order, may not be familiar with the accents. 'Give me, boy, two burgers there'. I have often waited a long time in the cab for an order to be understood.

One night, a passenger was trying to order some food, he wanted a number two, he then changed his mind and wanted a number

3, 'in fact, can you give me two number 3's' he says, now at that time, he was a bit drunk and he was also equipped with a strong Donegal accent.

The mistake can be easily made with the order. The person at the fast food joint replied 'We do not have a number 23 on the order board, what can I get you?', the reply was 'Two number 3's, with no pickle', 'you just want a pickle?' 'no, I want no pickle', 'that will be $11.25, go to the second window'. I always have trouble in these places he told me.

Anyway, he pays the money and is given the bag of food, when we move away, he opens it up to see did they give him the pickle or not. He gets a plastic box full of what appeared to be grass and lots of green. It's certainly not the two number 3's, that he ordered.

Flying.

The fastest and indeed the safest way to travel is flying. You might not think that, when you are going through turbulence, you're probably thinking of things you wanted to have done, before you died. There are over 10,000 flights every day and you only get to hear of the ones that crash. People say when it's your time's up to go, you will go. Someone once asked 'but what about if it's only the pilots time to go?' Now, that could be tricky.

I remember a few scares I had, during my years of flying, traveling from Miami to Boston. The Captain announced that we were going through a severe thunderstorm and not long after that, the plane is hit by lightening. The lights went out and the plane started losing altitude. It was some scare alright but the lights come back on again.

The captain, in the usually calm voice says, we were hit by lightening but as the plane is insulated, we can all rest easy. It's going to be no harm, but in the meantime, we are going to land in Philadelphia. Well, we landed alright but many people would not continue their flight, including myself. We were put up in a hotel for the night and completed the journey the next day.

Another time, when the plane was landing, it hit the runway fairly hard and the oxygen masks fell down. With all that was happening, some people were screaming but everything worked out alright. Landing and taking off are the most dangerous times during a flight. One evening, after a rough flight in a small plane, from New York to Boston, most people there were too scared to say anything, they were just thankful to be still able to stand up and walk away. The hostess thanks everyone for flying with them and said 'Now that you have completed the safest part of your journey, be careful out there, in that dangerous traffic'.

The safety statistics for flying are very impressive. I always remember what age you would live to be, if you were to live until you died from an air accident. If you were to live your life free of diseases, the odds are that, you would live to the ripe old age of 3000 before you would die in a motor accident. The odds are much better when flying, your average age for dying in a plane crash would be 1 million years old. Now, that's kind of comforting when you are going through turbulence.

When I travel, I still try and go the shortest possibly route. I do not believe in going six hours eastbound flight just to catch a five hour discount fare going west. A five hour journey that ends up taking seventeen or eighteen hours of travel is not much fun either.

I once asked my friendly travel agent for a cheap flight to Boston, one way would do. There's one on Monday from Dublin at £99 plus taxes. How about that? So I booked the flight from Dublin at 12.30 to go to London which was the first leg of the journey. My trip started when I got on a bus at 7.30am and went to Dublin. I got my 12.30 flight to London and arrived at 1.30. The Flight to Boston then was at 7pm. I checked in at 5pm. Too late, I was supposed to have checked in at 4pm.

Now, I had been waiting since 1.30 and ready to go. After begging to be let on the plane and not wanting to stay in London for the night, I was eventually let on. The flight was delayed for over an hour and it took off just after 8 o'clock. At 9 o'clock, the captain welcomes everyone on board and hopes everyone is enjoying their flight. We are now flying over South Galway on the West Coast of Ireland and that was 13½ hours after I had left Galway on the West Coast of Ireland. I was flying over where I started!

Next day I called my friendly travel agent for an explanation. I got it in a few words. 'What do you expect for £99. I hope you had a choice of dinner'. 'Yes' I said, 'a choice of feather or leather', which is normal now for airline food. I learned from that day on, you get what you pay for when traveling. I now travel only the shortest possibly routes.

Going To Church.

Going to church for most immigrants, well, is something that is done for a while after coming over to the States, but it soon turns into going to Mass just at Christmas and Easter and then seldom after that

Going to church has that little bit of Ireland attached to it, most of the priests are Irish or of Irish decent and one always hear people referring to something or another about the Old Country. The first thing you might notice would be the amount of collections, often three or more but always two, depending on the area you live in. You might be ready with your dollar, only to hear the crackle of paper and see for yourself, that people are now paying be check. You know, Visa and MasterCard will soon follow, you might even get frequent flier miles, now that's priceless. I expect this is called 'money given to improve your chances of a good place in Heaven'.

'Visa, it's everywhere you want to be', - How about Heaven!

Holidays In Ireland.

Holidays in Ireland are always good, just make sure you have lots of money when going there or else have none at all. Unfortunately, you probably will not qualify for free accommodation, food and money that are available to the 'new tourists' that comes to Ireland now. This new tourist just does not come over for the Summer, they settled for the long stay holiday and can be found at all the good resorts.

The ordinary holidaymaker in Ireland for the most part, does not go on holidays in Ireland anymore, they prefer to go to Spain or some other more exotic places other than Salthill, Tramore or Bundoran. It's regarded as less expensive to go to those places, where you are guaranteed sun, cheap drink and lots more of everything you might have in mind.

When you consider that, it cost €225 per person to go to the Galway races via helicopter from any Galway hotel, that amount would be about €50 more than a return flight to Spain. So, you would have even enough to eat for a few days as well, for what it costs to go to the races. Therefore, you certainly cannot blame people for going away for a week or two abroad.

Any seaside resort in Ireland now is just getting day-trippers and the weather has to be good, sunshine needed. The day-trippers are now generally women with a few kids, who drive forty or fifty miles for a few hours for their trip to the seaside. The man is left at home, which is often the best place for him to be because he has no sooner arrived, until he wants to go home again. Known at the seaside resorts as a 'come on, come on'.

Another visitor to the best places and who always wants the best views is the one that drives a camper or RV, the recreational vehicle, as they are known on the continent. Those people come with everything, they are self sufficient, no money or very little is going to be spent by that gang. Their RV's are equipped with satellite dish, a couple of bikes, a boat, dog and maybe even a cat.

Ideas And New Products.

You get an idea and you think that this should work well. Now, where to next, this process is called research and development and there's plenty of help out there for the entrepreneur. Well, maybe, but you had better be prepared to slow your plan down and you may be told we have some money available, if you have the product. Then, you will need a business plan that could take two or three months and four or five thousand euros to prepare. With all that done, you're going well now. You may even have plans for your premises, maybe in a business estate.

Don't ever build up your hopes too much because your great idea and product or service, might not be compatible with what is expected for that industrial estate or business park. Even before or during this time, you might even have considered taking out a patent for your product. Now, this is another slow and can be an expensive process, more money and sometimes you may have to wait years, only to be told 'Know Art', which means that there is something already similar on the market.

With all the help that's supposed to be out there, the best help of all is 'Just Go And Do It' yourself, you will probably have it done and up and running long before the business plan is complete.

Exposure on the TV is always good, The Late Late Show was always good. They have a show on one night each year for new inventions and services and this was a huge help to new business. Many people from all over Ireland put there wares on show there, myself and many more will be forever thankful to RTE.

Handcarts of Distinction.

This was another opportunity for me to appear on the Late Late Show. I had a display cart with old wooden wheels and a thatch roof on top to give it the appearance of an Irish theme and the cart was intended for the export market. A couple of days after it appearing, I got a call from a man in the drinks industry asking if I would be able to supply fifty hand carts. 'How would you like to see you carts at airports all around the world' he said to me. 'Our plan would be to put a cart displaying our products at fifty international airports, around the world. How long and when can you deliver?' 'I will need a week and I will be able to give you delivery dates then' was my reply.

After a week of frantic work, checking this and that, I worked out a staged delivery and price. I make my call with the details, looking for Mr. Big Order, but he is not available. 'When can I get in contact with him?' I asked. 'I don't know, he is not available' she said. 'I talked to him last week regarding handcarts for displaying of your products' I told her. She then told me, 'he is no longer with us, some of his decisions were not in the best interests of the company so he has parted company,' 'Have you heard anything about handcarts for displaying your products?' I enquired, 'No, but if you send on the details, it will be considered. Thank you'. Details were sent but that was the last of that dream.

The next outing for the handcarts of distinction, was at the world trade centre in Boston. There was a crafts show there and they were displaying many different crafts. Having a thatched roof on the cart looked lovely, now, what could be more Irish, well, not long after arriving in the building, what looked like a man with a lot of authority, asks for, (for wait for, this is good!) a permit to display and a certificate for the roof. 'I don't have any of them with me', I told him. 'Well', he says, 'you won't be able to display it without your certificates, that roof is a fire hazard'. 'A fire hazard' I said, 'Yes' he says, 'you've got to have a fire certificate' I told him that 'people in Ireland live in houses with the same kind of roof all their lives,'. 'I don't believe that, it's another tall story' he grunted.

I had to go and find the person in charge of the show and tell him the bad news that we are not going to be able to display the cart, without the fire certificate. He said to leave it to him so he went over and talked to the important man with phones and radios with a link to the Pentagon. He was not that hard to deal with after all, he said that no lights of any kind will be allowed on the roof. There was no need for any lights since there was enough lights around in the place to pick needles. So the display took place, without any further setbacks.

Mayfield Cork.

Back in the Sixties and Seventies, the only Irish people you would find in the Boston area were from Galway, Kerry and Cork. Now there are no barriers, they are here from every county in Ireland and everyone is proud of the country. They wear their county colors whether it's Tyrone or Wexford, it doesn't matter, they show their loyalty. Cork, now, they stand out probably above all the rest, that bright red jersey, wore with pride and passion, it does not matter what sport Cork is in, the support is there and it's massive.

One night, I was taking home this man and he had a lot to say. As usual, I would not have been listening to everything he was saying, as it was definitely the time to be 99% deaf. 'You're from Cork?' I said? 'Cork, Boy, you don't mind me calling you boy. Do you?', 'No' says I, 'Well, the driver earlier tonight got very angry when I called him boy'. I said 'why?' 'He was a colored driver and he said that his grandfather told him, before he died, don't ever let anyone call you boy. He was called boy for far too long when he was a slave and those days are long gone, no more boy now'.

I got him to his destination and he says to me 'And I, by the way, I am not just from Cork, Oh no, not just Cork, I am from Mayfield, the Republic of Cork.'

Soccer Teams.

In the late eighties, soccer for most parts was not heard of in the USA, a little of the game might be seen on some Latin American channel but that was about it. I remember one time, trying to talk to someone from Honduras, I asked him if he watched soccer, 'Yes' he says, 'you are from England?' 'Yes' I said because it would have made no difference saying I was from Ireland, we were not going to be discussing local issues anyway, so I let it pass at that. 'Big family play soccer' he says, 'some very good family, play soccer, all have same name. I love Sharp Family, very good, also candy very nice,' Whatever matches he had seen, there was no commenting and anyway he would not have understood the language.

Try explaining offside to him, I then asked him had he heard of Brian Robson?, 'yea, great player', Steve Bruce?, 'great player', Ray Clemence?, 'great player', Liam Brady?, 'great player', Mother Theresa?, 'great player'.

It was time to go. I had heard enough.

Video Tapes.

Even in the early Nineties, there was still not much soccer in the USA. Whatever little soccer there was on the TV would have come from some Mexican or South American, third or fourth division matches, from time to time. There was no Manchester United or Arsenal being aired in those times.

How things have changed in the last ten years. Now every day, either in a bar or on Fox Sport, you have live soccer, rugby, Gaelic football and hurling as it happens. In the late Eighties early Nineties, soccer videos and other sports videos were on sale in Ireland and Britain. Highlights of the season, match of the day and sports legends were all available, however, the only problem was that the tapes would not play in the USA. They were of a different format. Some people even went to the trouble of taking a video recorder from Ireland to the States to show the videos. In most cases, that did not work, first you had the different current, fixed that and then you had a TV problem.

The search began for a video that would show the different tapes and after some searching it was found and purchased. The business of transferring videos was started and it went well, especially around Christmas. The ideal present for many men would be a video tape of United, Liverpool, Arsenal or Celtic. That they could look at it, in the comfort of their own place. The one tape that outsold every other tape was that of George Best, nobody came near him in terms of sales and maybe in playing ability as well.

Voice Recognition.

I have thought for a long time about writing this book. A number of different things were holding me back, a major hold up was the typing of each story and the spelling. You can imagine my delight when I found out about voice recognition. This was going to be my savior, you just talked into the machine and it turned it into print, wonderful, I thought.

Off I go to Radio Shack, where I purchased this wonderful equipment. It turned out to be a computer disc with a headset, to make it look good. You read all the details and then started to teach the computer how to get used to your voice. You start off by reading from the computer screen and talking into the headset. Chapter one was about two pages long and when you finished you'd be thinking that the computer would recognize your voice by now. Well, no chance of that, there was a lot more reading to be done.

The next chapters I had to read were not as long but no more interesting and if you were getting angry or swore at it, you lost the few lines that you had already recorded. After about three and half hours of talking rubbish, the computer said that it was about 95% complete. To that, I said enough is enough and I clicked on the finish button.

Now, it was time for me to dictate my first letter to the computer so I said, 'Michael Lennon, South Street, Quincy, Mass'. I looked at the screen and read the following, Mikel Lenin, Russian Leader. This is supposed to be voice recognition, how are you!. I took disc and head set back to the man in the shop that had sold it to me in the first place. I told him, I spent three and half hours talking rubbish and this is what I got.

That poor man had a stammer himself and he says to me 'how, how, how, long do you think, think it, would take, take, take, to recognize me, me, me?' Forever, I would think, he then tells me that 'it's like, like a four year, year old, old, learning the Oxford Dictionary, not much good to me and many more.

This equipment was being sold as the answer to your typing problems, it just did not work, at that time. Now there's a new updated version. Does it work? I don't know, only time will tell.

Ireland.

The future looks good, prosperity is to be seen everywhere. The begrudges are having a bad time of it. Thousands of people that left in poor times have returned to build or buy houses, giving the country a great financial boost. However, a lot of the old traditions have gone by the wayside. Then again, the wren boys that used to be seen once a year are out every day in towns and cities performing 'The Fields Of Athenry'. Who knows, the All-Ireland Finals may even be played over a 5 match series, that would solve a lot of ticket problems.

You could have the first triplets ever to captain and win All-Ireland titles. D.J. Abu in Hurling, his brother Dara Thomas Abu in Football with MaryAnn Abu in Camogie. That is what the future may hold.

Taxi Epilogue.

I often listened to great ideas from people, ideas that someone will work on eventually and hopefully it will work out for them. As for myself, I would like to come up with something that would make life easier for every Taxi Driver, especially after closing time. A clip for the tongue, this no doubt would be a huge seller, a zapper type device that would let the tongue keep saying what it wants, but with no sound, how about that, it would even be a big hit for home use.

The next thing would be a new transport system, to guide anyone under the influence of alcohol home, probably something similar to a guide dog. Maybe, something a bit bigger, donkey size, now, this mode of transport would need to carry a tracking device linked to the home address. It would need to be programmed to find a way home, avoiding the bars and fast food joints. I think it could be done and I'm sure it should be done.

I have wrote a lot about carrying people who were drunk in the cab, they take up a very small portion of my work. When driving, and as I have said before, I am very well paid for what I have done. I have been given tea, coffee, bottles of water and bars of chocolate, by all the lovely people that I have picked up, especially the ladies that I have taken from one place to another.

I have even been invited to dinners at Christmas and Thanksgiving and often at 1am in the morning, I've been invited in for a cup of tea.

Thank you, Marty and indeed everyone else as well.

God Bless all of you,
Michael Lennon.

copyright © 2004 Michael Lennon

Just Go And Do It - Index

A Smile..2
Introduction...3
Quotes Of Interest...5
Ireland Of Today...7
School Days..9
Serving Mass...12
Jobs During School..13
The Bog..16
Bringing Home The Animals................................18
Cattle & Sheep Fairs..20
Extermination Of Vermin.....................................21
The Rosary..23
The Missions...24
Petrol Pump Money...28
The Television...29
Moving To Dublin..31
Arriving in Dublin..34
Jobs...36
Working in Birmingham.......................................39
Driving..41
Racers In The 70's...42
Driving In A Hurry...45
Water For Petrol..46
Windscreen Repair Service..................................48
Clocks...49
Mirrors..50
The Lotto Dartboard..52
The Reusable Matches..54
The Clapper..54
The Perfect Mouse Trap......................................55
The Eye Spy..56
Handball...57
The Vending Machines..62
Audio Cassette Machines....................................68
Video Games..68
Bumper Pool Tables...69
The Roller Skates..70

Concerts	72
Pitch And Putt	74
Bath Resurfacing	78
Football & Hurling All-Ireland Key-Rings	82
Gold and Silver Key Rings	84
Paper Library	85
Seaside Games Of Skill	87
The Rifle Range	89
The Cycle Race	90
The Cyclomobiles	91
The Great Race	92
Games At The Seaside	93
Selling Gold & Posters	95
Posters	96
Fortune Telling Machines	97
Candle Wax	99
Life Size Photos Of Famous People	101
Sand Art	104
Paint Like Picasso	105
Traveling To Festivals	106
Snooker Tables	108
World Snooker Champion	115
Weight In The Cue	117
Speed Systems	119
Umpire Assist	120
The Taxi	122
Arriving In The USA	124
Afraid To Eat	125
Immigration	127
Visiting The Uncle In The USA	131
Football And Hurling	134
Attacked	135
New Arrivals	136
American Women	137
The Big Dig	140
Driving Licenses	143
Drunk, In The Snow	145
Drunks	149
Life In The USA & Freedom	150
Late Night Runs	155

Late Night Runs In The Rain.................................157
Looking For Directions..160
People That Tell All...161
Permits..164
Opening A Business..165
Quick Marriage...167
See Who..171
Singing In A Cab...172
Snow & The Wrong House......................................173
The Airport Taxi Job...174
Taxi Driving..176
Elvis..183
Taxi Offers..184
Tour Of Boston...186
Where Do You Live? Schull......................................188
Best Wife In The World...189
Look Out For My Cat...190
You Talk Like My Father...192
Car Hire..193
Renting A Car Without Directions..........................197
Driving..198
Fast Food Ordering...201
Flying..202
Going To Church...206
Holidays In Ireland...207
Ideas And New Products...208
Handcarts of Distinction..210
Mayfield Cork..212
Soccer Teams..213
Video Tapes..214
Voice Recognition...215
Ireland..217
Taxi Epilogue..218

Cover Design & Book Layout By... Dan Hallissey

222

ISBN 1-41204368-9